D0153636

SAGE was founded in 1965 by Sara Miller McCune to support the dissemination of usable knowledge by publishing innovative and high-quality research and teaching content. Today, we publish over 900 journals, including those of more than 400 learned societies, more than 800 new books per year, and a growing range of library products including archives, data, case studies, reports, and video. SAGE remains majority-owned by our founder, and after Sara's lifetime will become owned by a charitable trust that secures our continued independence.

Los Angeles | London | New Delhi | Singapore | Washington DC | Melbourne

Advance Praises

———◦◦◉◦◦———

It is a path-breaking book on the youngest generation right now on this planet earth—the pre-teens and teens. No one has understood them the way Dr Sengupta has. He has decoded their mindsets, attitudes and behaviours and at the same time brought forth some very compelling aspects of their lives. Reading this book today will help us nurture a generation for the future. I wonder why no one wrote such books on us when we were growing up. Believe me, this is a must-read for everyone, and this book should be on your desk.

Syed Kirmani, *cricketing hero and legend;*
Padma Shri awardee; Arjuna Award winner; winner of
'Best Wicket-Keeper of the World' title

The Life of Z is a thoughtful book that brings into focus issues that affect Gen Z and shows how we can help nurture an extraordinary generation of achievers and change makers.

Ravi Venkatesan, *UNICEF Special Representative*
for Young People

The Life of Z is a fascinating journey that opened my eyes to the importance of Gen Z and the differences that digital transformation has brought to the way they think and operate. Gen Z are already the largest segment and increasingly our customers, employees and the future of society. *The Life of Z* puts the spotlight on this most important topic in the unique and engaging style of Debashish

Sengupta, which is both informative and academic but also creative. This is an important text that helps to understand the challenges and opportunities of Gen Z in a digital age.

Dr Alex Fenton, *Salford Business School, UK*

Once again, Dr Sengupta has been able to put into words the mindset of a generation. The aptly named 'zeners' or Gen Z hold the key to sustained success. This insight will help us change our business model so that we can attract Gen Z customers in the future. Hopefully, we have created a brand that these young people will be inspired to work for.

James Murphy, *CEO of Plant Happy & B Sustainable; Founder of the Lotus Awards, London, UK*

Dr Debashish Sengupta is a talented author, and this book proves to be unflinchingly honest, thorough, wholesome and extremely helpful. I can't imagine how challenging it would have been to write about Gen Z. It is an ultimate guide to everyone in understanding the art of getting along better with Generation Z, or as the author aptly calls them—'the zeners'.

Dr Padmasri Ayyagari, *MBBS, DGO, FRCOG, UK; MBA (Hospital Management); Obstetrician and Gynaecologist, Al Salam International Hospital, Kuwait*

Dr Sengupta has done it again. After *The Life of Y*, he is back with his trademark qualitatively abstracted approach to demystify and help appreciate the code, driving the generation referred to as Z. What is quite contrasting with his approach is something I have practised in my career: to stop trying to cure others and instead to try to care for them. I wish him lots of joy and happiness through this book. Hope this book helps improve the lives of many 'zeners' and their stakeholders.

Naga Siddharth, *CHRO and Head Teacher,*
Excellence, Vedantu; Curator at Measure.plus,
Bengaluru, India

Professor Sengupta has extended our understanding of the post-2000 born youth of our planet. This time, he has addressed the environmental and social factors that form their psychological traits and values pre-work employment. This helps employers, colleagues and marketers better understand the forming norms which have created the outlooks of these unique individuals.

Dr Bernard O'Meara, *PhD, Marquis Who's Who, Australia*

I heard Debashish talk about *The Life of Y* in Mumbai in September 2017. His expert knowledge of the subject was both infectious and enlightening. *The Life of Z* is a book of its time, one that will shine a light on how today's young people think, behave and see the world they live in. It is a valuable resource for us all.

Stuart Thomas, *Director, Masgroves, Birmingham,*
West Midlands, UK

After the success of *The Life of Y*, which has become a guide for many organizations and marketers to understand millennial behaviour, Dr Debashish Sengupta has come up with another gem—this time on an even more important and complex topic that will help parents, teachers, institutions and businesses understand and engage with today's pre-teens and adolescents. *The Life of Z* is truly the ABC of understanding this entire generation.

K. Sivakumar, *Co-founder and CEO,*
Saluto Wellness Pvt. Ltd, Bengaluru, India

It is a fascinating insight into the mind of the young, digital generation. This pioneering study provides its readers with awareness on what to expect from the first cohort that grew up with technology, enabling them to access and share information instantly and across the globe—and what has been the impact of this on Generation Z. It is an enlightening read for corporate readers, those in the field of education and parents alike.

Virpi Tarantino, *Executive Manager, Learning and Development, Oman Insurance Company, Dubai*

Gen Z is not just the label attached to a generation. It's quite simply the life, interests and future of those not very different from us as far as species go, but who could be from another planet in how dissimilar they are from us. Interestingly, they could even be our children—the self-appointed decision-makers we negotiate with every day and end up on the losing side of arguments with, too many times to count. So what makes them tick? What holds them back? How do they think; do they even think before they speak or act? What makes them smarter? If you think about it, they are our future consumers, whom we need to find relevance with. They are the opinion leaders of tomorrow. Love them, disapprove of them, question them, we first need to understand them. *The Life of Z* is an insightful and relevant deep dive into how this generation fits into our current reality and offers a new frame of reference to get to know them better: theirs.

Debashish unearths insights that lie just below the surface and interprets them with candour and humour to demystify an entire generation. In short, he does it again!

Priya Shivakumar, *National Creative Director, Wunderman Thompson, India*

The Life of Z seems like a really promising book. I look forward to reading it. Dr Sengupta's methods of simplifying deep research and presenting the story will make the book an easy but important read. We need a book like this one that expectedly gives us tools and frameworks to understand and deal with the unique behaviour of this Gen Z.

Roomana Basha, *Founder Ekdali.com;*
Freelance HR Consultant, India

The Life of Z is a one of its kind of book on the attitudes, behaviour and life issues of pre-teens and adolescents of present day, making the Generation Z or zeners as the author calls them. The book delves at length into the mental and physical health of children and the impact of digitization on these impressionable minds, which is absolutely invaluable. This book is a must-read for every parent, teacher, child counsellor, paediatrician and pretty much anyone who manages this generation. This is a gold mine for a steal you do not want to miss.

Dr Sandhya Rani, *Senior Gynaecologist, Apollo Cradle,*
Bengaluru, India

The most remarkable thing about this book is that it uses the voices of gen Z or 'zeners', as the author calls them, to make us aware of the huge responsibility bestowed on us to nurture and sustain a generation that is capable of bringing the change that we want to see in the world.

Marshall Goldsmith, The *New York Times* #1 bestselling author
of *Triggers, Mojo, and What Got You Here Won't Get You There*

Generation Z

Cyberjunkies

Informed

Zeners

Disruptors

Enterprising

The LIFE of Z

Changemakers

Vulnerable

Connected

Lonely

Curious

Influencers

The LIFE of Z

Understanding the Digital Pre-teen and Adolescent Generation

Debashish Sengupta

Los Angeles | London | New Delhi
Singapore | Washington DC | Melbourne

First published in 2020 by

SAGE Publications India Pvt Ltd
B1/I-1 Mohan Cooperative Industrial Area
Mathura Road, New Delhi 110 044, India
www.sagepub.in

SAGE Publications Inc
2455 Teller Road
Thousand Oaks, California 91320, USA

SAGE Publications Ltd
1 Oliver's Yard, 55 City Road
London EC1Y 1SP, United Kingdom

SAGE Publications Asia-Pacific Pte Ltd
18 Cross Street #10-10/11/12
China Square Central
Singapore 048423

Published by Vivek Mehra for SAGE Publications India Pvt Ltd. Typeset in 11/14 pts Minion by Fidus Design Pvt Ltd, Chandigarh.

Library of Congress Cataloging-in-Publication Data Available

ISBN: 978-93-5388-225-9 (PB)

SAGE Team: Manisha Mathews, Syeda Aina Rahat Ali, Ankit Verma and Anupama Krishnan
Illustrations by: Vaishnavi Vishwanath

Dedicated to the loving memory of
Tapasi

You are in a better place we know,
A place where there is no pain, no fear
A place where there is eternal peace, love and care.
We miss you and will only believe you are somewhere far away
Till we meet again you will be fondly remembered everyday.

Thank you for choosing a SAGE product!
If you have any comment, observation or feedback,
I would like to personally hear from you.

Please write to me at **contactceo@sagepub.in**

Vivek Mehra, Managing Director and CEO, SAGE India.

CONTENTS

———⊷◉⊶———

PREFACE

A radio buzzing in a corner, the transmission was unclear, the signal seemed to be wavering. I adjusted the antennae that we had fixed near the roof of the room. The voice on the side became better. By that time, I had repeated this ritual several times. However, the cracking commentary of the cricket match on the other side made up for all the hard work and irritation. Both my younger brother and I were stuck with the radio for the whole day. Our parents were not at home. My mother wanted to call our grandma and therefore she went to the post office to book a trunk call. It took few hours of waiting before her turn came and she could speak over the government-run public landline phone before returning home. We had the whole day to ourselves. It took longer than expected for our parents to come back home. They could not find a taxi near the post office and had to walk for nearly a kilometre before they found a transport. Poor mom, she had to cook the dinner after a long day. Meanwhile, India had lost the match. We spent the whole evening helping our mom in the kitchen. Another uneventful day had come to an end. But we had some excitement coming up. Sunday was just a day away when we would catch another episode of *Star Trek* and by that time we should also be getting a letter from my cousin brother who was sharing our secret encryption code, as he had promised in his last letter. This was to prevent elders from finding out the contents of our letter. And yes, he was also sending some photos from his recent vacation.

When I tell this childhood story of mine to my son, after listening to me with rapt attention, he tells me that there are technical flaws in my story. What? Technical flaws? I find his expression amusing; he finds it even more so. He asks me,

Why were you listening to the radio and not streaming live cricket over the Internet? Why did your parents go to the post office to make a call and not use their mobile to make a video call? Why did your parents not call an Uber instead of walking a long distance? Why didn't you order food over an app instead of letting your tired mom cook dinner? Why did you wait for Sunday to watch your favourite show and not stream it over Netflix? And why were you waiting for days for a letter instead of using WhatsApp or Instagram?

Not his fault. How will his generation that has been born in the cradle of technology and rocked by social media handles understand the times when we were children? They were born in a transformed world where on the one hand, rapid advancements in technology have opened the realm of possibilities, including space tourism, whereas on the other hand, the same technology threatens our very existence. On the one hand, the world has been brought closer than ever before with networks that defy limits of distance; on the other hand, it has been fragmented by economic, political and religious conflicts. Everyone has more friends than before, yet there is dearth of human-to-human connection. Today, they take more photos than Kodak films would ever allow, and share them on Instagram, yet they will never know the nostalgia of opening an old dusted photo album.

The first of the Generation Z natives or zeners (as I call them) were born in the year 2000, the first year of the new millennium. It has been 19 years since then and today they make up the largest percentage of the world population, slightly more than the number of the total number of millennials. A generational cohort that is the biggest chunk of world population and the one that has lived a very different time than ours during their formative years deserves both attention and exploration. They evoke a great degree of curiosity not only because they depict a completely different mindset and attitude but also because after millennials they hold the key to the future of this planet. Not to forget that zeners and millennials make up more than two-thirds of the total number of people whom you can count on earth.

This book brought me closer to this generation, and as I understood them and their life better, I saw homes, societies and institutions, which were not ready to accept, manage or engage this generation, become mostly defunct for them. The ironies in their life have made them confront with bane too wherever they searched for boon. They are powerful yet vulnerable. They can become the most influential generation that the world has ever seen yet could be lost in a waft of smoke, flamed by ignorance and arrogance.

We cannot afford this, and we know that. The only way out seems to understand this generation up close and personal and base our decisions of what we want to offer them on the foundation of real empathy. The findings of my research and my countless conversations with zeners, parents, teachers, private tutors, paediatricians, child counsellors, child psychologists and entrepreneurs have at times shocked, surprised and amazed me—all at the same time. I invite you on this roller-coaster journey, and I am sure that by the end of it you will know and see things very differently. Only then, our zeners can be real winners.

ACKNOWLEDGEMENTS

I am grateful to my wife and soulmate Vandana for not only being my pillar of strength but also going out of her way to help me in the most extraordinary manner without which this book would not have been complete in every sense.

I am thankful to the amazing women power of SAGE, my publisher. I would like to thank Manisha for continuing to trust my abilities and supporting me. She is not only the best editor with whom I have had the opportunity to work but she also has superb human qualities that make working with her a delight. I would also like to thank Shafina and Aarti for their relentless support, Anupama for the excellent cover designs and Ankit my production editor. I owe it to them all.

I am thankful to the amazing artist Vaishnavi—her sketches have pumped life in *The Life of Z*. She is insanely talented, one of the most creative persons I have ever met.

I would like to thank the countless people I met in the course of writing this book—parents, teachers, doctors, counsellors, psychologists and entrepreneurs who shared their stories and experiences with me. These guys rock and their lived experiences are precious.

I would like to thank my parents and family for sharing their love and care with me, always.

I would like to thank my son Arnab—he is the first zener whom I met. His love and innocence have been inspiration for this book. I would also like to thank my nephew Ayan. His smile is infectious.

I am thankful to my dear friends who have been like a ray of hope, joy and laughter. Their friendship has been very special.

And finally, I am thankful to the countless amazing zeners with whom I had an opportunity to interact. Each one of them is special in their own way. Their stories are incredible, the slice of life splashed on the canvas of this book. There are many more who may not have been mentioned in the chapters, but their inputs have added valuable insights to the book—Raunaq, Aaron, Amrutha, Madhulika, Indrakshi, Aarushi, Aditya, Aarush and many more.

There are many names that I am missing here, and if you do not find your name here, excuse me knowing well the limitations of human memory, but I want all of you to know how grateful I am for your support, encouragement and love.

1
THE NEW 'ZENERATION'

This morning while having breakfast, I burnt my tongue by accidentally sipping a steaming cup of tea. I blame it on my short-term memory. Today's breakfast at the office cafeteria consisted of delightful South Indian cuisine, including dosas, sambar, coconut chutney and, to top it all, a cup of hot tea. A second helping of 'dosa' and refilling of the tea cup was on the cards as the food was tempting. While sipping the second cup of tea, I forgot that it would be quite hot, poured directly from the flask, unlike the relatively less hot last few sips of the first cup. The short-term memory retention of the temperature of the last few sips of the first cup of tea is what made me subconsciously throw caution to the wind and take a careless sip at the second helping. Result—my tongue and throat experienced an immediate burning sensation that kind of spoiled my morning breakfast experience that otherwise I was enjoying till that moment. This just made me realize that memory can be as much of a problem at times as much can be the absence or lack of the same.

Remembering a good experience, good holiday, good people or good moments can be exhilarating and joyous. But remembering an ugly experience, people who have cheated you or hurt you, instances that have been full of sorrow or the feeling of losing someone can be troublesome, painful and stressful.

Remembering can be gainful but forgetting can also be blissful at times. From childhood, we teach our kids the art of memorizing

Generational Snapshot

Veterans

– Pre-World War generation

Baby Boomers

– Post-World War generation

Generation X

– Born between 1964–1965 and 1978

Millennials

– Born between 1979–1980 and 1999

Generation Z or 'Zeners'

– Born in 2000 and after

and try to make them good at remembering numbers, formulas, theory and techniques so that they can do well in their education and career. We must also teach them or rather train them in the art of forgetting things, people or instances that are not worth remembering, so that they can do well in their lives. At that moment, I realized that happiness is an outcome of both remembering and forgetting. Simply speaking, forgetting can be as powerful as remembering.

Talking about understanding differences in attitudes, mindsets and behaviours of different generations, keeping a fresh outlook towards the new generation, is significant. An attempt to fit the new generation in the old generational frame is akin to not forgetting and unlearning the past. Every generation displays a set of unique characteristics, attitudes and behaviours, more so if they have grown up in a completely transformed era. Generation Z, born in the year 2000 and after, are a fascinating and at the same time a very intriguing cohort. They are the post-millennials—the kids and teens of today in schools and colleges. They are nothing like the world has seen before and however clichéd this line may appear, the truth cannot be denied. 'Zeners', as I call them in this book, are offspring mostly of Generation X and few of them of early millennials. They have their dizzy highs as well as rock-bottom lows. On the one hand, they are highly confident, assertive, aware and ready to explore the world; on the other hand, they are swamped with life realties that threaten to annihilate them. All those with whom I spoke while writing this book, besides 'zeners', included their parents, teachers, private tutors, child counsellors, consultant child psychologists, paediatricians and even marketers. All of these listed here gave a very interesting account of this generation and at times seemed to be at loggerheads when it came to owning up the blame for what plagued 'zeners'. Nevertheless, what I am going to unfold in this book is an unbiased account, a never-told-before saga of Generation Z. So be prepared to dive deep with me into the 'life of Z' to discover their mind and who they really are, what they want, what they are missing and more importantly why they behave the way they do.

Let us begin on a positive, pleasant note.

Tilak Mehta, a thirteen-year-old entrepreneur and millionaire, is an incredible example and as you read his story, you cannot help but wonder how a thirteen-year-old boy could think and accomplish so much.

The Teenage Millionaire

Tilak Mehta comes across as another thirteen-year-old boy next door who loves to play football and badminton, goes to school with his younger sister Tanvi and studies in the 8th grade. But wait for him to start talking and his maturity will blow you away. He sounds much like a young entrepreneur who has very wisely invested in a start-up. And so is he, a thirteen-year-old entrepreneur, who founded the company Papers and Parcels in 2017. Yes, you read it right! He has become a household name in Mumbai, the financial capital of India, and has made waves in the national news. The nation calls him the teenage entrepreneur millionaire. He is our perfect Generation Z influencer or simply a 'zener influencer'.

Idea That Changed Tilak's Fortunes

A famous idiom goes as 'necessity is the mother of all inventions'. Tilak's story is no different, except that he created a company out of his experience. It all started in July 2017, when he visited his uncle's place in Borivali. He took his books along, with an intention to study. But as a teenage boy would normally behave, surrounded by his cousins, they became so busy in their play that he did not get time to study even a bit. So engrossed was this lad with his cousins that he even forgot to bring back his books when he returned to his home in Ghatkopar. His home was almost 25 km away from his uncle's place in Borivali, a journey of close to one and a half hours to two hours depending on the traffic. He wanted his books back the same day as his exams were approaching and he had to go for his tuitions. However, despite his best efforts, he could not get his books back the same day. A same-day courier service would be too costly. He had no option but to wait for his books. This long wait for his books made him realize that many in the city would be facing the same problem that he was facing at that time. One day, while returning from school, he saw a man wearing a white shirt, white pyjamas and white 'Gandhi topi (cap)'. Unmistakably, he was one of the famous Harvard case study-featured 'Dabbawallas' of Mumbai.

Tilak stopped to quiz this man about his services and charges. Back home, a little maths told him that it would not cost anyone more than ₹40–₹50 every day. Dabbawallas, the famous tiffin service in Mumbai for office-goers, connect the cooks with the corporate executives who prefer home-made tiffin over outside food. Hence, typically a Dabbawalla would pick up tiffin carriers from doorsteps of the women cooking food at their home and getting the tiffin ready and deliver the same to various offices. Later, they would collect the tiffin carriers and drop them back. Hence, the two transactions on the same day would cost less than a dollar. 'That was cheap', thought Tilak. He discussed this with his dad and reasoned why the same couldn't be done by a courier company. He got a long explanation from his dad, most of which he could not understand by his own submission.

However, the thought did not
leave his mind. He kept thinking
why he couldn't do something
similar for the society, more so
at an affordable price. The idea
of Papers and Parcels was born.

Tilak continued his research.
Armed with some data, he
shared his business idea with
his uncle Ghanshyam Parekh and
with his father. He envisioned a courier company that would do same-
day deliveries in Mumbai at a cost that will be just about a quarter of
what normal courier companies would charge. His efforts finally paid
off with his family showing faith in his idea. His uncle decided to quit
his job and join him in creating a unique company. Thus, Papers and
Parcels was born.

Getting on the 'Train'

The next two and a half months saw an intense effort to discuss
the idea with Dabbawallas and tie up with them for the pick-up and
delivery of the couriers. The model was complementary to their
original tiffin's business. Besides, 'Dabbawallas' were known for
their efficient supply-chain management and low-cost operations.
Tilak recounts how it got extremely difficult to find the right person
among the association of 5,000 'Dabbawallas', since they operated
with a highly flattened organizational structure. Finally, they could
find the right person, who was Mr Subhash Kalekar, the spokesperson
of the 'Dabbawallas'. This however did not resolve Tilak's problems
immediately. His age became his biggest barrier. No one outside
his family, including Subhash Kalekar, took him seriously. Tilak adds
that he was at times politely and at other times very curtly told
that he was still a 'bachcha' (child) and how could he help someone.
Persistent efforts by Tilak eventually made Subhash believe that he
meant business and to finally give him an appointment to visit and see

them. Tilak utilized his first meeting with Dabbawallas to understand their way of operations. He requested Subhash if he could travel with them on one of the days and experience their operations. He was in turn quizzed if he had travelled in a train before or had travelled in a local train with overcrowded coaches, where if you could not find a place to stand, you would have to find an object to hang on somehow. Tilak had never experienced either of these, but he decided to take it on. The next challenge was to convince his parents that he would travel alone with 'Dabbawallas' in a train and to different parts of the city. Although not completely assured of his safety, his parents seeing his determination allowed him to make this audacious journey. The day started at 7 AM and by 8 AM they had picked all the 'Dabbas' (tiffin carriers). The train journey in a Mumbai local was a mind-boggling experience for him. This journey did two things to him—first, the 'Dabbawallas' were convinced that he was serious about his venture; and second, he became more convinced about his venture and its economic viability, besides the social impact that it would generate.

Train to Train-ing

All this while, Tilak kept thinking about how he could make the life of the 'Dabbawallas' easier and make their services faster and even more reliable through integration of technology. After tying up with 'Dabbawallas', the next step for him was to take them from 'train to training room'. Tilak, who studied business and information science at his school, Garodia International Centre for Learning, Mumbai, was well conversant with technological aspects. He and his uncle trained the 'Dabbawallas' on how to use technology for business, operations and soft skills. Presently, they had 300 'Dabbawallas' signed up with them. Besides this, Tilak's company hired 180 of their own associates. So, in total, they have an army of close to 500 associates on the ground, picking up and delivering couriers on the same day in Mumbai city at a price that was a steal, making life of 'Mumbaikars' (a general name coined for people residing in Mumbai) easier every day.

Unlike traditional courier, Papers and Parcels, as a company, picks up couriers from the doorsteps of the customers. The customers use an app to book the services. A live-tracking feature, same-day digital receipt as a proof of delivery and complete background tech-based monitoring of operations make Papers and Parcels' offering secure and attractive to its customers.

Drive with Passion

Tilak's passion for technology and his enterprising nature knows no stops or should we say no pit stops, for he is now developing a miniature Formula One (F1) car. Once this is developed, he will develop a prototype and then the actual model. He is planning to replicate the same in the F1 car to be used in the school competition of F1 cars introduced the last year. F1 in schools is a unique way of offering a way to learn science, technology, engineering and maths (STEM) and perhaps the only global multidisciplinary challenge in which teams of students aged nine–nineteen years deploy CAD/CAM software to collaborate, design, analyse, manufacture, test and then race miniature, compressed-air-powered, balsa wood F1 cars. Tilak seems to have found his own formula for now.

The Young Visionary

Tilak picked up important management lessons from 'Dabbawallas'. It is amazing how this young boy of all but just thirteen years could gather so much wisdom to capture these insights. Teamwork, time management, commitment, an incredibly flat organization and the respect for food that the 'Dabbawallas' demonstrated impressed Tilak so much that he incorporated all these principles in his company and its culture.

Papers and Parcels works on the very same principles and has immense respect for the parcels that they deliver, knowing well how important they were for the people who were sending and receiving them. Tilak is also honest to acknowledge that his experience about logistics has grown since he started his business and has even started contributing his knowledge in further improving his company's services. He states the relationships that he has developed with his employees, Dabbawallas and his customers as the USP of his business.

Profit-making is not his priority, and he has a vision of making Papers and Parcels the best courier company in the nation, providing employment to 2,000 people in Mumbai by 2020 and gradually having a pan-India presence for his company. Tilak is a learner, and it is evident from the fact that he used to accompany his father often on his business trips when he was even younger. He recounts two such quotes that he remembers even today and these words have struck a chord with him.

The first one is 'When others see walls, I see doors' by Mr O. P. Jindal of Jindal Steel and Power and the second one is 'We believe in results and not in reasons' by none other than his dad.

Tilak follows these two like gospel truths and has learnt to 'see opportunities and not find excuses'—something similar to 'one who has will will always find his way'.

Tilak Mehta's story is enough to fill us with amazement and we cannot help but feel inspired. But Tilak is not alone. It will not be an exaggeration to say that 'zeners' are born influencers, out to change the world. There are no two words about it. Shubham Banerjee (of Braigo fame), Lakshya Subodh, EvanTubeHD, Gabe and Garrett, KittiesMama and Ryan ToysReview are some more names of an endless list of 'zener' influencers.

This is the most disruptive generation the world has ever seen and has the power to change the society and the world in significant ways. They are less tolerant of the status quo and instead of cribbing about the world's problems, they would rather pick up the broom and 'clean it'.

K-Innovation

A recent National Sample Survey revealed that 33 per cent of Indians live in houses whose area-is less than 580 sq. ft. More than 60 per cent of such houses are covered with furniture, leaving very little space for the occupants. Space-saving furniture are a welcome solution and the only hope for such residents to decongest their houses. Bed SI is one such innovation—a foldable structure that can be spread as a sofa, bed or table depending on the need and can be stowed away when not in use. However, the biggest surprise is yet to come. Hold your breath, for the developers of this innovation are not IVEY graduates but two 4th grade students—Renee and Tanmay—of an international school in Bengaluru.

How many of us remember what we were doing when we were in the 4th grade—probably reciting poems. That's the only thing I remember, reading my favourite poem at that time—'Timothy Boon'. But here are two 'zeners' winning first prize at the Bangalore Design Championship. In an age for balloons, chocolates and toys, these two amazing kids are preparing for large-scale production of their innovation, which will cost a shade above $30–$40.

Mindfulness

A fifteen-year-old Jain Balmuni or child saint recently performed an extremely difficult and complex procedure called Avdhan. Padmaprabhchandrasagar, as he is now called, memorized 200 questions and their answers in a chronological order. Not only this, he can actually answer any question randomly from the lot.

All the audience has to do is to ask him the question number. This prompts him to recite the question and the answer. The teenage boy has become 'Maha Shatavdhani' after performing this act, a feat rare among Jain monks. The questions and answers range from Jain scriptures to mathematical equations, synonyms, antonyms, foreign phrases, auditory and sensory inputs. Such memory is possible though rigorous training that builds a peaceful mind and enhances concentration in the process. 'Avdhani' is a rare procedure attempted by few Jain monks. To think of a fifteen-year-old boy performing the same is nothing short of a miracle.

Information boom and social media are just the right enablers that help them propagate their message in an unprecedented manner. However, such abilities swing both ways. They can be immensely constructive as well as outrageously destructive. Given the right opportunities and their energies channelized in the right direction, 'zeners' can transform the world and the universe. However, left unmanaged, the same environment can exploit their intelligence and ability, leading to most undesirable outcomes.

They have also grown up in the aftermath of 9/11 and 26/11 and have seen/are aware of ongoing terrorist extremism. On the one hand, globalization is lowering national boundaries and making the world more multi-cultural and multi-ethnic. On the other hand, religious fundamentalism across the world, growing politics of hate, growing intolerance and violence, recession, unemployment and underemployment of millennials are also on the rise. The start-up culture, changing world economic dynamics with India, China upstaging the USA and other Western countries as the fastest-growing economy of the world, increase in per-capita income along with increasing inflation—the environment could not have been a more eclectic mix of positives and negatives loaded in almost equal proportions.

Digital Dilemma

'Zeners' are living in an era of digital revolution. They have been born in the cradle of technology and are growing up in a world of apps and social media dominance. The world has shrunk into the mobile screen, and one touch is all you need to communicate with the world. On the one hand this has meant unhindered access to information and access to cutting-edge technology that enables them to learn better and create. F1 in schools that Tilak was talking about is the only global multidisciplinary challenge in which teams of students aged 9–19 deploy CAD/CAM software to collaborate, design, analyse, manufacture, test and then race miniature, compressed-air-powered, balsa wood F1 cars. The idea is to inspire students to use information technology to learn about physics, aerodynamics, design, manufacture, branding, graphics, sponsorship, marketing, leadership/teamwork, media skills and financial strategy, and apply them in a practical, imaginative, competitive and exciting way.

Ten Minute Hacker

Emmett Brewer is an eleven-year-old boy from Texas who hacked into the replica of the Florida Election results website and changed names and replicas in less than 10 minutes. DEF CON security convention organized a hacking competition for the six- to seventeen-year-olds to identify the security lapse in the electoral website. Emmett was the fastest among all the participants. Interestingly, the US department conducted this sort of competition only for the 'zeners'. With

suspicion of Russians hacking into the US electoral websites, the security 'holes' demonstrated by Emmett's hacking will go a long way in making the US electoral system more robust.

Tech Sleuth

Another teen from Mumbai tracked down her phone and the person who stole the same using technology smartly. After losing her phone, Zeenat Banu Baig signed into her Google account using another phone and kept tracking the 'My Activity' section of her Google account. One day, the thief booked a train ticket for himself and also took a selfie. He also took screenshot of the ticket. Using her Google account, she tracked down the ticket that the thief had booked as well as his photograph. She handed over both these crucial pieces of information to the police who arrested the thief very soon.

On the other hand, the same digital technologies can be a headache for most parents and teachers. There is health risk associated with overexposure to digital gadgets that even doctors have corroborated. Too much digital is also ruining the real experiences of the 'zeners'. The virtual is taking over in a big way and many times making them believe that the virtual is real. The virtual world of digital games and online games is potentially dangerous in many ways, offering tremendous ways of exploiting them.

When a fourteen-year-old Mumbai boy Manpreet Singh Sahani committed suicide reportedly as part of a deadly online social media game called the 'Blue Whale Challenge', it raised many questions. This was not an isolated incident. The deadly game invented by an expelled Russian psychology student, Philipp Budeikin, claimed lives of many kids across the world between 2016 and 2017. A 50-day online game, which started as a free will game but over a period of time resorted to bullying, threats of harm to near and dear ones and many such consequences if the player did not complete a series of tasks that were linked to self-harm, ultimately drove them to claiming their own lives. Why would these young teens and kids fall prey to this game? There are no easy answers. Media reports suggest that twenty-two-year-old Philipp Budeikin, the creator of the deadly game, said in an interview in St Petersburg that his resolve was to 'cleanse society by provoking people who think they are not worthy of being alive to commit suicide'.

Sounds scary, isn't it. Budeikin may be one of those psychopaths who are out to harm young unsuspecting people. However, even more worrisome is the fact that many kids became vulnerable to this online game. And if reports are to be believed, the Blue Whale Challenge is not the only such online suicidal game. There are plenty of those such as F57 and Wake Me Up at 4.20 am. The online abuse of children is on the rise in India. Specifically to the Blue Whale Challenge, the number of calls on the national child helpline managed by the NGO CHILDLINE India Foundation has risen by close to 400 per cent in the past three years since 2015.

How could an online game influence the kids more than their parents, teachers, friends and well-wishers? Many such questions lie unanswered. The only way to find answers to what's behind such unexplained behaviours is to understand the attitudes and mindset by uncovering the layers that make up a generation.

Take, for instance, online behaviour; there is a very interesting difference between the online presence and behaviour of baby boomers, millennials and the kids and teens of today called the Generation Z, born in the year 2000 and after, or 'zeners'. For baby boomers, who saw the internet only when they were in their mid-forties and social media when they were past their fifties, going online is an effort and has definite login and logout times. In other words, they log in to their online accounts for a definite period of time, spend some time and then log out. Millennials, on the other hand, remain connected at all times and have a seamless existence between the online and the offline world. For them, both the worlds co-exist, and they 'check in' into one without really 'checking out' from the other. However, when it comes to 'zeners', for them the virtual world is the real world. For them, playing an online game is not just gaming, it is real—the friends that they meet there are real for them, and the culture of these games is also real for them. The virtual is slowly becoming the real for the 'zeners'. That is how they are interpreting. The unreported impact of massively multiplayer online games (MMOG) on this generation is huge. That perhaps explains the Blue Whale syndrome, at least from a peripheral behavioural perspective. We still need to dig deeper to manage such behaviours.

Informed Hard Nuts or Argumentative

They are not an easy generation of kids and adolescents to manage. Parents and teachers often find themselves challenged while managing the 'zeners'. Perhaps every generation's parents would tell the same story about their kids, but this is not as similar or simple as this appears. 'Zeners' have an unhindered access to information, thanks to the internet and social media. They are extremely knowledgeable and can surprise by their knowledge that can often put a grown-up adult to shame. In general, their IQ levels are quite high. Research evidence also supports the fact that IQ scores have risen dramatically in the past 50 years worldwide, more so in the developing nations. But does that mean that generations are getting smarter as well? 'Zeners' are also found to be highly argumentative and difficult to persuade and can be called 'informed hard nuts'. They use logical persuasion and at the same time cannot be persuaded with anything other than logic or rationale. What does all this talk about the 'zeners' reveal and how does this affect their equation with older generations?

'Short' Notice

Amrutha is a teenager, a fifteen-year-old girl, who lives with her parents and younger sister in Bengaluru. She does not find herself and her parents on the same page when it comes to her choice of clothes, a fact that she finds a bit bizarre, funny and at times irritating. She likes wearing shorts that none of her parents approve. Hence, she does not get to wear them outside her home, but with some cajoling, she has managed to convince her parents to wear them at home. She often finds her mother reminding her that when she was young, she used to wear those kind of shorts concealed by long skirts and not just wear them and roam around, the way she does. Amrutha adds, 'I wear them because they are so comfortable. I do not understand the hullabaloo around the same.' Maybe it has to do with the kind of difference in approaches that she and her parents have. She finds her parents always very dignified and formal in their conversations, while she is more of the casual type. 'While we do respect each other's choices, at times things are really bizarre', adds Amrutha.

Her mother constantly urges her to keep company of 'brainy' people so that she also thinks and behaves more intelligently. When I tell her that she is quite brainy herself, Amrutha smiles and with a sparkle in her eyes whispers, 'My mom does not think so', and we both break into a laughter. She goes on to narrate a particular incident that was both hilarious and annoying for her. A send-off lunch for a cousin who was going to the USA for studies took all of them to a restaurant.

I like 'churidars' too, but I prefer jeans more. That day I was dressed in a pair of ripped jeans, and my mother started giving me those stares which made me contemplate whether I was dressed in an odd manner. It was not like a torn pair of jeans but just a ripped one like a stripe near the knees. We were coming back from lunch and were in our car. My dad was sitting next to the driver, and my mom, my sister and I were sitting on the rear seat. When we stopped at a traffic signal, my mom suddenly started screaming in excitement, 'Putty, Putty, Putty' (she calls me putty at home, a nickname she often uses). She pointed out to a beggar at the signal who was also wearing a torn pair of jeans. The way she said that, it seemed that something drastic had happened. I said,

Fine, you can make fun of him, but then even he is a human being, isn't it? He may be wearing it because he has no other clothes to wear and I am wearing it because it is trendy, so what's the big deal in this? I do not find any shame in the fact that we are wearing a similar pair of jeans.

That was the end of the conversation. Amrutha and her mother didn't ever discuss this topic after that. However, Amrutha prefers wearing shorts these days at home only. She loves her parents but is still not convinced with their sermons on choice of clothes. But she signs off with a smile, 'We can always agree to disagree.'

What does Amrutha's story tell you? Are they unmanageable or is there something we are missing out in understanding how to manage this generation? Remember that this is going to be critical in deciding how much we can connect with them and engage them to ensure that we can raise them in a way that does justice to their zeta potential.

Learning or Knowledge—Game of Probability?

Talking about the potential of 'zeners' and the task of managing them, teachers in schools who are encountering this cohort every day also face this challenge. 'Zeners' are extremely curious, love experimenting and are bubbling with innovative and creative ideas. They are passionate about their pursuits and want to convert their passion into their career. But do they get an opportunity to do that? Do we as parents or teachers or the larger society provide them that opportunity or the canvass to let them paint at will or are we cocooning them into the traditional shell of what success means to us? What does success mean to 'zeners' after all?

A radio jockey (RJ) on a morning radio show was advocating that exams should be enforced on school kids from the 5th grade onwards, and the ones who flunk should not be promoted to the next grade. The fact is that most schools in India have exams for kids from the kindergarten onwards. The zealous argument put forward by the RJ and advocated by many in this country and in many parts of the world is that most of these tests are testing knowledge and not learning. The percentage of marks received by the student, often touted as the most important milestone by parents and teachers, do not guarantee an assurance of learning. 'Zeners', a curious and highly informed generation on the other hand, is seeking learning not knowledge or mere information. Information is anyway abundantly available. They are growing up in the age of voice assistants such as Amazon Echo Alexa and Google Home who can provide any information by a simple voice command. Do they really need schools for 'collecting this information'? After talking to countless teachers, visiting various schools, reviewing board curriculums and talking to 'zeners' and their parents, it essentially boils down to a choice between the present pedagogy routine in schools and this new generation's quest for learning and education that can be tailored to life experiences.

Traditionally, coming first or second in a class has been a matter of pride for the parents when it comes to their kids' school performance. But then aren't we subjecting kids to unfair comparisons by ranking their performance? We keep saying that each child is unique and has his/her own set of capabilities and talent. Yet we compare them subjecting the majority to a feeling of inferiority, further demeaning the whole meaning of education and learning in their eyes. Many may disagree with such a viewpoint, but at least for now Singapore seems to be determined to make learning fun for every child and not turn it into a competition. Singapore has decided to eliminate school exam rankings while retaining some form of benchmark and information to help students understand their relative performance and know about their strengths and areas of improvement. Information, such as class and level mean, minimum and maximum marks, underlining and/or colouring of failing marks, pass/fail for end-of-year

result, mean subject grades, overall total marks have been dropped from the report card. Qualitative descriptors of performance are being chosen in place of quantitative description of a student's performance. Henceforth, teachers will continue to collect information about their students learning through discussions, home tasks and quizzes. Stress will be on making learning free of competition and making the students learn self-discipline that they need to face their life's challenges.

Clearing the Air

What Varun, a teenager and a 12th grade student, has achieved is seldom taught in schools. Varun Ramakrishnan has collaborated with a 51-year-old data scientist to develop a computer-based sensor device that monitors the air pollution levels using laser sensors installed at various locations across Whitefield in Bengaluru. This zone known for its feverish industrial activity has posed a big challenge to the residents of this area with worsening air quality day by day. With the state department failing to provide air quality data, these two have developed the AirCare network which is a low-cost device and completely crowd-sourced. Their data have exposed the worst hit pockets of the area that need urgent attention—one of them being a hospital area that has been worst hit. The presence of a graphite factory in the vicinity has ebbed the air quality level to dangerous levels. No wonder the hospital has been increasingly getting cases of cough, allergies and coronary heart problems, among others. Varun is using his self-acquired knowledge to solve a real-life problem.

The teachers whom I spoke to could easily be divided into two distinct categories—one who were hyper-critical about their students and mostly blamed parents for the behaviour of the kids that they found hard to manage; the other who seemed to appreciate the unique attributes of this generational cohort of students and took responsibility for their actions. The 'zeners' whom I spoke to, all had their favourite teachers as well. From all these discussions, one thing was crystal clear—the teachers who made learning fun not only found more favour among the 'zeners' but also found it easy to manage them and their behaviours, while the others who followed more traditional pedagogy routines evoked low interest among the students and at the same time found it difficult to manage the 'zeners'. The fact that is still of concern is that the percentage of the latter group of teachers is significantly more, and most of the good practices of the teachers are individual-initiated rather than being organization-wide accepted practices. Pertinent questions, therefore, loom large on the horizon—Are our present-day schools, schooling system, curriculum design, and teaching principle and pedagogy suited to the needs of this hyper-intelligent and hyper-informative generation? Should schools be knowledge hubs or learning ecosystems? Are schools shaping the 'zener' talent and incorporating right behaviours and life skills? Do we need the traditional schooling system at all? What is the role of teachers, parents and other stakeholders in the new transformed learning system?

We will need to find answers to these questions, else we risk blunting the sharpness of the 'zeners', turning them into finished pieces produced by mass productions, all of whom look and behave alike. It is time to take a call as to what kind of legacy do we want to pass on to this generation.

Progressive Iconoclasts

Zeners have grown up at a time where they have seen increased hate-based politics that divides people in the name of religion, region, ethnicity and language, and even extremism in the name of religion. They have seen heated debates about LGBT rights and call for social justice. Have 'zeners' fallen prey to such divisive politics or embraced inclusivity and diversity? What is their view of hate crimes and wars in the name of religion and ethnic backgrounds? Will the world be one or many in their hand?

License to S-Kill

Mithi Jethwa, a sixteen-year-old girl, is playing a pivotal role in the rehabilitation of Maoists in Odisha, an eastern state of India. Having lived in an area infested with Maoists during her father's tenure as a senior police officer, no one better than Mithi knew the importance of amalgamating the Maoists with the mainstream youth. Her efforts have paid off, and she has been able to impact a major policy change.

The new policy has dropped the minimum qualification needed by surrendered Maoists to join the governmental Indian Technical Institutes (ITIs). Joining an ITI is mandatory for the former rebels to learn a vocational trade and earn a monthly stipend of ₹6,000 for three years. This has tremendously increased the number of former Maoists joining it and preparing themselves to get an employment later. Mithi got an opportunity to interact with Maoists when she accompanied her elder sister, a teenager herself, who had worked on a project, 'Naxal Terrorism—Cause and Remedy'. It is then that she learnt that most Maoists do not have education till the 8th grade, which was earlier the minimum qualification requirement for joining it. Mithi's efforts are drawing accolades from all corners.

So, are the 'zeners' developing a Zen view? Will they change the strained relationships across the world, relationships between human beings that have been obstructed by racial, regional, religious, cultural, linguistic and economic slurs? If most 'zeners' are like Mithi and her sister, then this generation holds a hope for a better world. It will be interesting to explore the impact of their environment on 'zeners' and how that has shaped their view of the world around them and beyond.

Convoluted Relationships?

While they are busy trying to rebuild broken human relationships, their own life relationships seem to be in a sort of tumble. Or at least that is what I understood from my initial interactions with this cohort. So I decided to dig deep and find answers to some key and pertinent questions concerning their relationship dynamics. Are 'zeners' missing out on real relationships?

How can a fourteen-year-old boy have had four break-ups and be in a fifth relationship? Many suggest that there is a certain amount of isolation that 'zeners' exhibit in their behaviour. This is not to suggest that they are frivolous when it comes to relationship, but there is something that prevents them from understanding the essence of real relationships and emotions. They are becoming too mechanical or robotic when it comes to relationships.

Is it the emotional shielding by the parents who overzealously try to prevent them going through emotional turmoil or is this the digital age of 'move on' that is making them devoid of these real relationship experiences? Many suggest that although this generation is extremely intelligent, they lack empathy. A research by Professor Brett Laursen of Florida Atlantic University, published in the *Journal of Research on Adolescence*, shows that differences in submissiveness increases friendship instability, especially among boys. Increased competitiveness lowers submissiveness that ups the chances of confrontation in their interaction, leading to destabilizing their friendship many a time. Does that mean that 'zeners' have created a 'zone' for themselves when it comes to relationships that allows selective 'access'? Why are problems of bullying on the rise among school children? These are the questions we need prompt and correct answers for.

Another area of concern, when it comes to relationship dynamics among 'zeners', is the rise of abnormal sexual behaviour. Some reports and research studies seem to suggest that sexualized behaviour in very young children is on the rise. Why is this problem related to sexual behaviour among kids becoming a growing concern? Is easy access to pornography fuelling such behavioural issues? In a shocking incident that occurred in July 2018 in a village near Dehradun, five boys aged nine–fourteen years, reportedly raped an eight-year-old girl after watching a porn movie on a mobile phone. The cold-hearted planning and execution of this crime is what should worry us more than anything else. The boys lived in the same locality as the girl and knew that she stays alone in the house for few hours every day. They lured her to vacate the house and committed the crime. These boys were from a rural area, not from a metro city, and it would be wrong to assume that pornographic content on mobile phones is limited to cities. The kind of impact such content is having on impressionable minds is terrible and the outcomes such as this one are often horrific. There are conflicting opinions though on how much sexually explicit material, especially pornography, can turn on sexually aggressive behaviour among kids and adolescents and whether it makes them believe that consent for such acts from the opposite gender can be assumed, rather than being sought. We will need to dig deeper. Considering that consequences can be absolutely destructive, it needs serious exploration.

Another problem growing rapidly is the issue of teen pregnancies. The statistics show a steep rise in such cases. According to the data collated between April 2016 and January 2017 by the health department's Mother and Child Tracking System (MCTS), pregnant girls under the age of 18 numbered at 59,717 in Karnataka, with Bengaluru Urban having reported a maximum of cases (8,099). This was followed by Belagavi (6,416), Mysuru (3,500) and Ballari (3018) districts. These statistics clearly show that this is not limited to urban centres alone. Other reports confirm similar trends in the rest of India as well.

Some doctors believe that the main cause is ignorance about the consequence of an experiment stemming out of curiosity, the 'cool' factor or sexual abuse, many a time provoked by content promulgated by internet sites and social media. What is really behind such rising cases of teen pregnancies? Do pregnant teens or their boyfriends usually inform their parents? Are these also leading to unsafe abortions? How is all that impacting teen health? These and many such questions need to be answered.

Don't Be Judge-Mental

'Zeners' are kids of Generation X and early millennials who were brought into the modern-world cut-throat competition and the so-called race. Are they passing their genes and behaviour to the 'zeners' as well? Do 'zeners' suffer from a lowered self-esteem?

When a teenage boy tells me during an interview that marks are the only measure of success and those who fail to get good marks are considered numskulls, it is really concerning. He further adds that parents compare them to other kids, teachers compare them to other students in class, and the relatives and distant friends seem to be more concerned and inquisitive about their secondary and higher secondary board results. Is there too much pressure on 'zeners'? This hard squeeze is manifesting itself in the form of worsening mental health, depression and anxiety, leading to increasing cases of school shootouts and suicide at teenage. Reports like a sixteen-year-old boy killing himself because his father refused to buy him a smartphone while his friend had one, a fourteen-year-old boy ending his life at not being elected the class leader or a thirteen-year-old girl hanging herself to death for being slapped at school for not completing her homework are enough to fill us with horror. No reason is a good reason for someone killing themselves. Are the people around them making a mistake of thinking that these reasons are very petty and completely mis-calculating how the kids could be processing the same incident in their minds? Are these reasons reported in news? Recent 2018 data from the NGO CHILDLINE India Foundation report 14 million 'silent calls' on the child helpline in the past three years. Data also show a sharp increase in such calls year after year. 'Silent calls' are likely to be children or even adults who may call back again and can indicate a troubled child or a child in distress. The NGO report also clearly shows that calls seeking emotional support and help due to stressful family situations like divorce of parents or dysfunctional homes are on the rise. Jayadeva Institute of Cardiovascular Sciences and Research in Bengaluru, the biggest cardiac care hospital in Asia-Pacific, admits 150 young heart patients every month that even include teenagers. In fact, 5 per cent of their patients are below twenty-five years of age. That's huge when considering teens and young adults. Should this not concern us to find out why our kids are becoming stressed and suffering from mental and physical health disorders? It is important to explore the causes, effects and solutions to such stress-related disorders.

Cutting the Mustard

Irrespective of how we slice a generation, each generation brings something unique on the table that is often intriguing. Understanding the same forms the basis of managing and engaging them in a manner that is constructive for them and productive for the world.

'Zeners' are a fascinating cohort to study. They are highly informed and ridiculously intelligent, and prefer learning over knowledge and want to follow their passion to explore the unknown and go beyond the obvious. Yet they face some unique challenges where they often find people, institutions and the world around them pulling them in directions that are often different and dare I say contrarian.

2

BOATS IN THE OCEAN

———

It was 21st of June and I was sitting frozen by the news that I had just watched on television (TV). A teenage girl in her 10th grade was found in the girl's restroom of her school with her wrist slashed and bleeding profusely. She passed away while she was being taken to a hospital. Another suicide, another youth died. The school where this incident had happened was supposedly one of the famous brands. Like every other news, this was the headline for one day, mention for another day or two and then buried under the pile, forgotten and forlorn. But deep within every such tragic news is a greater tragedy that no one cares to see or know. It just cannot be another story. I decided to scrape the surface. Speaking to few students of the same school, I discovered that she was a studious girl and extremely well-behaved. While other students were preparing for their 10th grade board exams, she had already finished her preparation for competitive exams for higher studies. However, she always seemed to be under pressure, according to her classmates. She had reportedly confided to her close friends the immense pressure that she was facing from her parents. She had faced this right from her childhood, the pressure to perform and be number one in academics. And so she had, throughout her schooling. She always stood first in all her classes. She always came to school, even if she was not well. If she ever got one mark lesser than any other student in her class, she would get severe scolding from her parents. In the 12th grade, the pressure had grown. Coercion from her parents was a regular affair. She could not participate in any extra-curricular activities or sports. She hardly had any social life. Her parents wanted her to gain admission to the Indian Statistical Institute (ISI) at any cost. She would often break down in the class. That day, she excused herself from the class at around 1:30 PM to go to the restroom. Neither the teacher nor her classmates noticed her absence till about an hour. It was when a search operation was launched that one of her classmates found her sitting on the floor of the restroom, unconscious, both her wrists slashed, a polythene bag on her face and blood all around. It was too late. In the suicide note that she had left behind, she had written that after 'this', she would not have to see the angry, scolding faces anymore.

What would the parents do now? It was easy to make a villain out of her parents. Undoubtedly, they would have to accept the lion's share of the blame. But it is also true that their lives would be completely gutted after this incident. While others would forget, they would relive this day every day from there onwards. They would suffer more than one can ever imagine. During all those years, did they ever realize that in their desire for superlative performance from their daughter, they were pushing her way too much, over the edge, to a point of no return? To be fair to them, perhaps they never did just like many other demanding parents. Perhaps the severe depression that the girl was going through was never detected by the parents.

It is this obsession with academics and academic performance that does many in. Parents often argue that they as kids faced similar coercion and pressure to perform well in their studies and since they survived those parental incursions, their kids would too. But then there are many things that most people, including most parents, do not understand about this generation. One, this generation is an extremely high potential generation and, second, they are not as emotionally resilient as one may expect them to be. This is not to suggest that they are delicate; it just means that they need to be handled with care. The environment is responsible for it, and parents who have been emotionally shielding their kids ever since their birth are also responsible for the same. We will talk more about the same in the later chapters that describe in detail how the dynamics in the home and outside are changing and how they have impacted the mental health of this generation.

Research proves that this generation has a very high potential. Psychologists have long known the role that genes play in our intelligence. But do generations also play a role in our intelligence? Do subsequent generations become smarter? Thanks to some new data from a longitudinal study that we might have a better insight. Researchers from the University of Aberdeen and the Scottish health board NHS Grampian in their research found an IQ difference of 3.7 points between the two generations, but after the age of sixty-two the difference jumps to 16.5 points. Another research found that the IQ difference between generational cohorts grew significantly over the course of 50 years. In short, research proves that newer generations are more intelligent.

But this high potential and high intelligence of the current generation is often confused with being limited to academic excellence. For ages, intelligence has been confused with the ability to master academic concepts and perform well in the examination, enough to outperform the competition and earn coveted university degrees. This was never true and becomes an even bigger myth when we talk about Generation Z or the zeners. Armed with better intelligence and exposed to the floodgates of information and global media, their potential and possibilities are no more limited to academic grades. Instead, they have the potential to shine in any field, provided it matches their passion and interest. All they need is support to pursue their dreams and guidance to channelize their energies.

During the course of my research, I found enough and more evidence of the same.

Living a Dream

Jannat Zubair Rahmani, popularly known as Jannat, has a social media following enough to make people feel dizzy. She has over 5.6 million followers on Instagram and 14 million followers on TikTok; she is the first in the country to hit 10 million followers on the TikTok app which made her famous as the TikTok Queen.

Born in Mumbai and a native of Lucknow—the city of nawabs—Jannat is blessed with talent and style in equal proportions. It will not be wrong to call her a teen icon, who has already worked for more than 11 years in the TV and film industry.

But for Jannat, her beginning was not as dreamy as life is for her now. Her father was the one who recognized that she had a flair and talent for acting before anyone did. She recalls how her father used to take her for auditions and she would do nothing, and he would take her back home. This practice continued for more than a year, but her father did not give up. He would never scold or pressurize Jannat for not performing well during the auditions. Patience, perseverance and belief of her dad paid off finally when Jannat's hidden talent was recognized. She got her first break as a child actor in a TV show *Chand Ke Paar Chalo* on NDTV Imagine channel. Her work won her more TV shows—*Kasturi, Dill Mill Gayye, Kashi, Phulwa, Haar Jeet* and *Maharana Pratap*, to name a few. She became a household name with her show *Phulwa*. Her performances won her the 'Best Child Actor' award at the Indian Telly Awards. Although only seventeen years old, Jannat, owing to her talent, got a show as a female lead for the TV fiction drama *Tu Aashiqui*. This won her the Youngest Achiever Award at the Gold Awards in 2018.

Jannat vouches for the unstinted and relentless support of her family in making her one of the most exciting young talents to look out for in the Indian TV and film industry. She has never gone to a shoot alone. Her parents have sacrificed their own interests to ensure that she gets to do what she loves most—acting—and live her dream. As she has to appear for her 12th grade board exams shortly, she finds time to study on sets. With the help of her private tutors, support of her parents and her own dedication, she is marching ahead with confidence.

Jannat has appeared in applause-worthy roles in few films. Her music videos are ready to be released soon. And she is looking forward to her first big break in movies very soon.

In her own words, 'When my fans write on social media things like "You are my inspiration," "You are my idol," "I want to be like you," I feel that I must have done something right.' Be it her official app Jannat Zubair Rahmani Official or her YouTube channel Complete Styling with Jannat Zubair, she does everything with equal aplomb.

Jannat signs off by saying something that is worth reflection, 'Parents should support their kids in following their passion. There are already a lot many pressures on the child. Instead of adding more, parents should help their children to overcome them.'

Jannat's advice for parents is not misplaced. When she refers to other pressures, she is referring to the peer pressure and societal and contextual pressure to perform and prove oneself continuously in a world of Instagram, where nothing remains in one's private domain. The support from Jannat's parents has helped her succeed in performing arts. But she is not an isolated example.

A Girl with a Paint Brush

Kamakshi is the youngest Mandala artist in the country, says the latest entry in the *India Book of Records*. She is all but five years old.

Kamakshi's father, Sudhanshu Basandani owns a pharmaceutical business. During our discussion, I discovered that Kamakshi's mother Mukta Basandani was a fantastic artist herself. Kamakshi's feat at this tender age was not a planned mission. For Mukta, engaging her toddler Kamakshi in various kinds of colouring and paper crafts started as a way to keep her busy. Mukta did not want her daughter to go down the same route as most kids of her age were going through—the smartphone route. She had seen so many parents using smartphone or TV to keep their kids busy and engaged. But that was not her cup of tea, nor did she want her daughter to be busy for the sake of it.

Mukta noticed that Kamakshi took unusual interest in colouring. She gave Kamakshi whatever she found at home like empty glass bottles to paint. She made sure to take time out to guide Kamakshi, who made beautiful artworks even in that tender age.

Coincidentally, during those days, Kamakshi was gifted a Mandala art book by one of her friends. For the uninitiated, Mukta says,

Mandala is complex abstract design that is usually in a circular form. Mandala is a Sanskrit word meaning circle. Mandalas usually have a centre point, from which emanates an array of symbol, shapes and forms. Mandalas can contain both geometric and organic forms. Mandalas colouring books are used for meditation. Doctors suggest these books to pregnant ladies, those who suffer from depression or anxiety. It has a lot of benefits for kids as well. While colouring Mandalas, concentration power in kids increases, handwriting improves, patience level increases and they become more creative. When Kamakshi got this gift, we thought it would be too much for her considering her age. Drawing mandala is a very complex art. It involves drawing a lot of concentric circles and lines to create blocks. Once the blocks are ready, designing in them can be started. It may take a few days to complete one Mandala. But we were surprised to see that not only with a little guidance Kamakshi started doing Mandalas really well but also that she displayed unusual patience in completing her artwork.

Mukta took Kamakshi to a Mandala workshop looking at her interest in the art form. She was the youngest as a four-year-old to attend the workshop. The workshop further added to her zest for Mandala. Mukta was surprised to see that while adults found it difficult to finish a Mandala art piece in one session, Kamakshi would sit at one place for four hours, refusing to leave till she completed her Mandala art piece. Her concertation and persistence received constant motivation from her parents Mukta and Sudhanshu.

Over the weeks and months that followed Mukta could see Kamakshi taking deep interest in Mandala art form. Whenever Mukta used to profile Mandala artwork, Kamakshi would want to know more about the choice of colours and design.

During a visit to her gynaecologist, Mukta presented the doctor with a Mandala artwork made by Kamakshi. The doctor was naturally very impressed. But she advised against simply distributing the artworks made by Kamakshi. She was the first person who told Mukta that those artworks were of high quality and they should consider organizing an exhibition of artworks made by Kamakshi.

Mukta kept thinking of the suggestion that her doctor had given, but she was not sure if it was a feasible idea. She found her pillar of strength and support in her husband, Sudhanshu. Through their efforts they were able to book the most revered exhibition centre in the city of Jaipur, Jawahar Kala Kendra. Considering the age of the artist, there was a lot of interest among the media as well.

Days running up to exhibition were filled with nervous excitement for both Sudhanshu and Mukta. Kamakshi, blissfully unaware of the big moment that awaited her, enjoyed her moments under the sun. Her parents ensured that she did not feel any stress whatsoever in terms of having to prove herself to the world. They decided to use the exhibition only as a vehicle of motivating little Kamakshi. They knew that once her artwork was exhibited, most people would find it difficult to believe that a five-year-old could make such breathtaking artwork. Hence, they made a short video of Kamakshi making Mandala paintings.

The first day of the exhibition was filled with excitement. Gradually people started walking in. Media was very impressed with Kamakshi's work. The video of Kamakshi making the Mandala paintings was played with the help of a projector at the venue. People and the media were very impressed with the video. It created a lot of believability factor for Kamakshi's work. A couple of foreign tourists who visited the exhibition had high words of appreciation for Kamakshi. She also interacted with the visitors but was shy of speaking to the media. Sudhanshu and Mukta ensured that Kamakshi did not feel the heat of public and media attention. She was left to play in the kids' area of the exhibition venue. Most of the conversation with the media was done by Sudhanshu and Mukta, with Kamakshi only adding small bytes from her side. The turnout on the second day was huge. After the first day of the exhibition, the media's extensive coverage created a flutter in the city and loads of people came in to see the paintings. Many parents brought their kids to the exhibition. The exhibition proved to be very successful and Kamakshi was inundated with offers for conducting Mandala workshops for other kids.

Kamakshi today holds a record in the *India Book of Records* for being the youngest Mandala artist in India. She also won the Naari Shakti Awards. These awards are given to honour women who have done extraordinary work in their field or have been an inspiration. Kamakshi is the youngest recipient of this award. Interestingly, Kamakshi's mother also won the same award a few years ago. The only difference is that Kamakshi won it at the age of five years.

But it is not only the award or Kamakshi's record that is worth mentioning in this story. There is a lot to learn from Kamakshi's parents. Despite all her spectacular achievements, both her parents Sudhanshu and Mukta have decided to give Kamakshi the freedom to decide whether she wanted to pursue the Mandala art form in the future or not. As she grows up, if her interest shifts to something else, they have decided to support her in her new quest in the same way they supported her for the Mandala. Mukta recalls that being not as good in academics as her other siblings were, her greater proficiency in arts never found too much acceptance as a child. Like other children, she had to pursue something that she never really wanted to and found little time to pursue what she was passionate about. As a mother, she does not want Kamakshi to face the same dilemma while growing up. Instead, she should be able to do and pursue her dreams uninhibited. Also, success makes parents insecure about their children's future and they want them to continue following the tried and tested 'formula'. But Sudhanshu and Mukta on the other hand have not let the early success of Kamakshi come in the way of her pursuance of dreams.

Boy Wonder

Ricky Patel became a household name when he starred with the cinematic legend and millennium icon Amitabh Bachchan in a movie called *Bhoothnath*. The cute child became the centre of attraction. He achieved this rare distinction at a young age of all but six years. Thereafter he starred with another huge Bollywood star Salman Khan in the movie *Tubelight*. More Bollywood films followed. Today, about ten years old, Ricky has achieved what many dream all their life.

But all this was a distant dream not so long back. It was not only Ricky's talent but also the ability of his parents to identify this talent when he was a toddler, their wisdom to take him to right places at the right time and now their sacrifice in lending their unstinted support to Ricky at the cost of their own comfort that has propelled Ricky to stardom. Having said this, it is worth noting that while conversing with Ricky's mother I realized that they are not glamorized by this world of cine-blitz and have ensured that Ricky enjoys his childhood; his work is just a way to give his talent wings and not a vehicle to realize their unfulfilled dreams or for achieving their own life's milestones. That is what makes Ricky's story worth narrating.

Ricky's parents hail from a small sleepy village near Indore, a city in the central part of India. The village was so remote that they didn't even have manually drawn rickshaws for transportation in the village. However, an amazing part of India's growth has been the revolution of communication technology that has ensured that even the remotest village in the country, which may still not have access to all the basic facilities, still have communication gadgets and technological infrastructure to support the same. People may not have a permanent roof on their head, but they have a mobile phone and small TV in their home. Ricky was fascinated to watch Amitabh Bachchan delivering his iconic dialogues on a popular TV show. He insisted on learning the poetic dialogue. His parents were amused since it was a long dialogue and they thought it would be difficult for a four-year-old child to learn such a long script. But to their surprise, they found that he not only memorized the long dialogue but was able to recite it with the right expressions. Ever since, it was his dream to meet the Bollywood superstar.

At the age of five, Ricky won a fashion show contest in Indore. His ramp walk and his ability to mouth the iconic dialogues mimicking the Bollywood legend won the hearts of the judges and he won the first prize. Utterly impressed, the organizers suggested his parents to take him to Mumbai, the epicentre of the world's largest film-making mecca, Bollywood.

Ricky's parents did not ignore the advice and during his winter vacations, they took him to Mumbai. His mother recounts how stepping into this huge city made them anxious and wonder how they would be able to manage in the huge metropolis. They hardly knew anyone in the city and had no connections with the world of cinema. They visited some studios and walked into some random auditions which were being organized. One of such auditions given by Ricky was of Balaji Telefilms, arguably the number one production house in India when it came to producing TV series and web content, a fact hardly known by Ricky's parents when he was appearing for auditions. After giving auditions, Ricky along with his parents went back to their village near Indore, as Ricky had to attend his school. After about 10 days, Ricky's father got a call from Balaji Productions informing them that Ricky had been selected for the grand TV series *Jodha Akbar* based on the life of the Mughal emperor Akbar. They requested Ricky to be brought to Mumbai for a 'look test'. That same day, they took the evening train and next morning they reached Mumbai. Ricky has not turned back since that day. He has moved from strength to strength and charmed the TV and film audience, alike, with his innocence, confident performances and immaculate ability to mouth long dialogues. Ricky's mother adds with pride that the day Ricky's first show was telecasted on TV, no one could be seen on the village streets. Everyone was glued to their

TV sets. Ricky was an overnight star. Pankhuri, who is the creative head at Balaji Productions, recalls how confident Ricky was when he faced the camera for the first time. According to her, Ricky showed so much promise in every shot that he won everyone's heart on the sets.

Ricky was not only winning hearts on the set, but he was also winning off it. His mother says,

Ours was an inter-caste marriage and both our families refused to accept us and our relationship for a long time. But because of Ricky, both the families forgot their ego and animosity. They accepted us and we are so happy about it. Ricky has been an angel in our lives.

The word 'angel' is not exaggerated when it comes to Ricky. I personally had the most delightful experience interviewing him. He was such a sweetheart. He has worked with some of the biggest stars of Bollywood, the likes of legendary superstar Amitabh Bachchan, Salman Khan, Akshay Kumar, Shah Rukh Khan and Ayushmann Khurrana. However, despite all the success, Ricky remains the boy next door and has retained the innocence of his age with a dollop of charming sweetness.

Over the past few years, he has done TV series, movies and dozens of TV commercials. Ricky by his own admission enjoys doing his work. His mother recalls the first time Ricky met his dream star Amitabh on the sets of his first movie. Ricky was just six years old at that time and he realized his dream of reciting the dialogue of the baritone star in his presence. Also, Amitabh was reportedly delighted to see such a small boy reciting the poem written by his late father.

However dreamy Ricky's run may appear, it was not without its own share of trials and tribulations. Ricky's parents, who come from a small place, had more people around them who demotivated them and even scared and warned them against taking Ricky to Mumbai. Some termed the move useless; others warned them that Ricky would get spoiled in the glitzy world of glamour and fame. Some told them that they did not know how to speak English and would get heckled in the new city for their rustiness. Ricky's stay in Mumbai meant that his parents would have to live in separate cities. Till date, Ricky's mother stays with him in Mumbai, whereas his father stays in Indore, his place of work. Some of their acquaintances cautioned them that such long-distance relationship could result in strains in their relationship and lead to cracks in their marriage. Despite all these dissuasions, Ricky or his parents have not given up on their dreams and continue their persistence in the city of dreams. Ricky's parents however have not let Ricky get burdened with work. They ensure that he has time for his studies and play and can have a normal childhood like any other child.

Ricky, although just ten years old, carries a wise head on his shoulder. He wants to go to a film school abroad to learn direction

and animation when he grows up. He loves his parents and signs off with a message for other parents. He tells me about one of his friends who wants to act like him, but his parents are not allowing him to do so. They just want him to focus on his academics. 'Please let your kids pursue their dreams. Do not force them into doing something that they do not want,' Ricky signs off.

I wonder how sometimes kids know what we adults struggle to understand.

Flooded with Words

Subhashish Dey is a fourteen-year-old wordsmith who has published a fictional novel *Fate's Design*, which held its position on Amazon top 100 books of its category for many weeks and has received appreciation from none other than the iconic movie star and legend of Hindi cinema, Amitabh Bachchan.

Subhashish recalls how writing of this novel began in the November of 2018. They were living in Chennai, a city in the south of India. The unprecedented rainfall in the city led to flash floods. He, along with his parents, was stuck in his house. All schools and offices were shut down. It used to rain the whole day. Although, their apartment being on a relatively high land and their flat being on the first floor, he and his family were spared from water havoc in their house, there was no electricity, limited food supplies and no Internet for many days. He just had a laptop that he could charge at a common charging point in the building run on battery. During this adversity, he hit upon the idea for his novel. When I asked him how he got the idea for the story, he smiled and told me that he got it in his dream. That sounds even more impossible. No wonder scientists have not been able to solve the secret behind human dreams till date. On a more serious note, he utilized the time at home and his idleness to write the first draft of his book. When Chennai was getting flooded with water, he was getting flooded with ideas. By the time the water receded, and life started limping back to normal, he had created a masterpiece.

Subsequently, the manuscript underwent several rounds of revisions done by his father Dr Subhendu Dey, a business management professor. Dr Dey's experience in editing came handy. The ready manuscript was mailed to several publishers but sadly there was no response. Dr Dey by his own submission admits that at one stage he thought that it was perhaps too ambitious for a fourteen-year-old boy to send the manuscript of a novel to big publishing houses. But soon after, they heard from Good Times Books who agreed to publish the book. The book was published few months later and accolades started flowing from all directions. The book has an amazing plot with complex sub-plots. Reviews from all and sundry were superfluous, something that neither Subhashish nor his parents had ever imagined. National media coverage, testimonials from people of repute, recognition among peers, recognition from his school and the love of the readers, he has got it all.

Subhashish grew up in a house of educationists. Both his parents are in the profession of teaching. His mother Chaitali is a mathematics teacher with a reputed school. At home, he always found himself surrounded by books. When he was a toddler, his mother used to read him stories like many parents do; however, as he grew up, his interest in reading also grew. Chaitali recalls, 'I was working in this school. Subhashish was in grade two. He had to wait an extra two hours for me to finish my work before we could return home. Those two hours every day, Subhashish used to just read.' As he grew older, he started writing short stories, something that received a lot of encouragement from his parents, particularly from his mother. When he finally wanted to expand his canvass and write a novel, his parents always believed in his idea and creativity.

Subhashish wants to become a doctor when he grows up but also wants to continue his passion for writing. In fact, he is already working on his second novel. Besides being an author, he is a pianist and a painter. He has a long way to go and Dr Dey aptly signs off by saying, 'Our job is to keep supporting him and we will keep doing the same. We will support him in his ventures provided he shows committed and persistent efforts.'

A common thread that runs across all these real-life stories is the role of parents. In all these cases, the parents had something in common. They looked beyond just academic performance as a gateway to the future of their kids. This is not to suggest that there is anything wrong with being academically gifted. But everyone cannot be Einstein just like all fingers cannot be of the same size. So why try to make an Einstein out of a Picasso. Further they trusted the potential of their kids and let them explore the realms without expecting miracles overnight or putting any undue pressure on the kids. They provided support and guided their kids to wade through the water, rather than trying to launch a lifeboat for them. Take Jineet Rath for instance. Jineet credits his success to his parents. Having parents who support your dreams and let you pursue them, instead of burdening them with their own dreams, is a blessing. Jineet is lucky and blessed to have such parents whom he calls in his own words 'super-supportive'. They recognized his talent very early and allowed him to do what he loved the most. He also describes his school as one that is extremely supportive. Being a regular student, he gets support and flexibility that helps him manage his shots without compromising on school work. Jineet is already a star but he is a teen worth looking out for in the future. He might become a huge movie star.

Jineet Rath has the rare distinction of working with all three ruling Khans of Bollywood. He is a teenager who has acted with Aamir Khan in the movie *Talaash* and with Salman Khan in *Tiger Zinda Hai*, and he was there at the D'Décor app launch event as co-launcher with Shah Rukh Khan, besides playing the young Hrithik Roshan in the movie *Guzaarish* and with Shahid Kapoor in *Phata Poster Nikhla Hero*. If this is not impressive enough, then Jineet has acted in an Oscar-nominated movie *Dam999*.

Jineet's modelling career started when he was only six months old. Yes, you read it right! The story goes on something like this— Jineet had gone with his parents to EsselWorld, an amusement park in Mumbai. A random person started clicking his pictures. Confronted by his dad, the stranger revealed that he was the director of a very prestigious advertisement agency and he wanted Jineet to model for a global kid brand. Jineet's parents initially did not like the idea as they were concerned about such a young baby going through the stress of shooting. However, when they were assured that he would be in good hands and the assignment would in no way stress their child, they allowed him to do the commercial. He became the Huggies baby and overnight he became the cutest baby in the town whose photos were on Huggies packets, billboard advertisements and TV commercials. Many other ad campaigns followed, including Life Insurance Corporation of India, Aviva and Amul Cheese, to name a few. He displayed talent and inclination towards acting from a very young age. At the age of ten, he got his first TV soap *CID*, which was at that time one of the longest running TV shows in India. More TV soaps such as *Shapath* and *Maharana Pratap* before movies happened and Jineet became a child star. He realized his stardom for the first time when during a school parent–teacher meeting he ended up signing so many autographs for other parents and kids that his new pen ran out of ink.

The more I met zeners and their parents, the more I was convinced that this generation is made of a different mettle. But it is also pertinent to remember that there are ironies that we need to understand. On the one hand, they are extremely intelligent and have high potential. On the other hand, they are also emotionally vulnerable and susceptible to stress, anxiety and depression. While they grasp things very fast, they are not amenable to conventional learning styles. They are talented, and the theory of multiple intelligences applies thoroughly to this generation, but if not allowed to pursue their passion and follow their interest, they might just log out. There is no middle path or compromise for them. If supported and guided properly, they can touch a new sky. On the contrary, if left to the scourge of the world, they can be lost to the depths of abyss. They are gifted; yet, they do seem to lack the gift of introspection and self-reflection.

They, like any other generation, cannot be treated like any other generation. They need to be understood as a cohort by anyone who manages them or tries to reach out to them. Before writing this book, I spoke to countless zeners (both kids and adolescents), their parents, grandparents, teachers, child counsellors, child and adolescent psychologists, paediatricians, private tutors and even entrepreneurs designing products targeted towards this generation.

Speaking to one such mother, her comments were not to be taken lightly. Sumana Chatterjee, the mother of a thirteen-year-old girl, said,

This generation is not in touch with their inner self. It is not their fault. They have been born in an age of Instagram and social media that influence their life. They are too busy to show oneself better to the outer world. This competition leaves no time for them to self-introspect and self-reflect. They do not really know at times what's special about them. I feel they might make life choices that they might regret later. My daughter is academically good, she is a prefect of her class, she is good in sports, good in dance. She will have to know what she really wants to pursue in the future. But for that she will have to do self-exploration and I see my role as a mother to help her do the same.

Perhaps Sumana is right. In the chapters to follow, we will try to understand this generation and their attitudes, mindsets, behaviour and preferences. We will also try to understand their unique life context and the complexities that come with it, examining it layer by layer. I have always believed that empathy and good understanding precede engagement. Although we will explore solutions as well, this book should not be seen as a panacea or a magic fix. This book is a serious attempt to build a deep understanding about this generation to enable the stakeholders to search for their own solutions as well. So are you ready for this journey? All I can tell you is that it is going to be a very interesting ride, like this generation itself. So come on, let's dive in.

3

How Did the Zebra Get the Stripes?

The Young Scientist

Akash introduces himself as a human who is ten years old, about to turn eleven, one who likes physics and biology, and hates the idea of his mother leaving him alone at home for long and the fact that his father has yet not acceded to his request for a pet dog. Akash, who is a homeschooler and who wants to be a scientist at a space research agency when he grows up, seems already to be on track of fulfilling his dream. He has got the rare honour of being the only child to be invited by the prestigious National Center for Biological Sciences (NCBS), Bengaluru, to spend some time in its labs every week and learn from the scientists themselves.

Akash, whose mother is an English teacher in a well-known school in the city, has been homeschooled from an early age. He feels lucky to have parents such as his, as they have given him the freedom and space to do

what he wants to do. He says, 'My parents understood from an early age that I was very curious and that is why I was homeschooled.' He feels that in schools, the curiosity of the kids is constricted as they are not encouraged to ask questions. If someone asks more questions, then they are labelled as the 'dumb' ones.

A typical day of Akash is very different from that of most kids. While other kids scurry off to school in the morning and follow a set timetable once they reach the school, Akash decides what to study that day in consultation with his father every day. He then spends his day reading about the day's topic from a vast array of books that he has, which include textbooks, science books like *Brief Answers to the Big Questions* by Stephen Hawking or even university books, or his YouTube teacher teaches him when he logs in. One of his favourite YouTube channels is PhysicsHelps. Other times, he goes for a leisurely morning walk with his mother or plays with a fancy breed dog in the neighbourhood, who has inspired him to know about genetic engineering.

I decide to probe him a bit to test if he really means business when he tells me about studying university-level books. And he becomes tremendously excited. He drops names such as Lagrangian mechanics, partial differential equation, second order differential equation, quantum mechanics, general relativity and neuroscience, and starts explaining what he is studying in these topics. I must quickly withdraw as all that he was explaining to me sounded too complicated.

On the surface he is like any other ten-year-old kid. He is a dog lover and wants to do his bit to help the stray dogs on the streets. He wants to save the world by working on climate change. He loves playing football. He also has a cracking sense of humour and keeps me in good wit throughout the interview. He jokingly adds that he is a karate white belt. But once you talk to him, know him a bit, you see him displaying a maturity that is rare for his age. He is focused and knows the importance of being invited to the prestigious labs of Professor Sumantra Chattarji and Dr Shashi Thutupalli of NCBS.

Akash seems to have gone in-depth of the subjects that have struck his curiosity instead of studying a vast array of subjects like we did at school and then trying to figure out at the end of the schooling what he wants to become and then choose the arts, science or commerce stream for his graduation. Is the approach that Akash and his parents have taken correct? It is difficult to comment, but Akash seems quite happy at being allowed to make his choices as to what to study from an early age.

The story of Akash raises several pertinent questions. Is traditional schooling losing its relevance when it comes to this new generation whom we call Generation Z or 'zeners', as we call them in this book? Is Akash a gifted child and therefore his parents are homeschooling him? How come Subalaxmi, the mother of Akash, who herself is a teacher in a mainstream school does not believe in the same concept of schooling when it comes to her own son? Clearly, the discussion cannot be over without speaking to Subalaxmi.

Subalaxmi is an English teacher in a well-known school in the city that belongs to a big brand of school chains in the country. She has been in this profession for close to 12–13 years. Being a senior English teacher, she was very eloquent in her conversation that made my job so much easier. What she told me affected me to the core and hence I reproduce here a verbatim copy of what she told me.

She started by making a very interesting remark,

Like every parent, I put Akash in a school, like every teacher parent I admitted in my school. I felt very happy that we will be able to travel in the school bus together. In fact, when Akash was just a tiny baby I had made a lullaby for him that also had lines in which I said that I am waiting for the day when Akash and myself would go to school together. My wish that my child comes to school with me was very strong. And I have been a teacher in a mainstream school for close to 13 years. If a parent such as myself would decide to withdraw my son from the school and homeschool him, then it must be quite a decision.

I couldn't agree with her anymore. My curiosity increased further. Subalaxmi went on saying,

Frankly, regular schooling didn't work out for Akash. It does not work out for most kids whether they are gifted, or not. In my case, I saw this as a clash between the values and priorities that I had as a parent versus the value and priorities of the school and the society. My core value tells me that creativity and freedom are the most important and letting my child explore them is my biggest priority. Whereas a school that has 45 kids in one class, for them discipline comes first and foremost. I also wonder how our traditional schools work would, if all kids want to explore, run around. The way they function, soon it will become chaotic if they let kids explore. That is why we find teachers saying 'Keep quiet', 'Do not move from your place', 'Sit down in your place', 'Do not talk now', 'Wait till I finish before asking a question' and 'Sit straight'. Continuous instructions by teachers create adults who are good in taking instructions, know how to fit in the system, but lose a lot of spontaneity and creativity right at the beginning. A simple test for this is that you go to any primary class and ask for 5 volunteers and no less than 15 would rise up from their seats to volunteer. However, you go to any senior class and ask for students to volunteer and not even two students would raise their hand. The reason is very simple; they have by now grown up and been conditioned by the system that does not encourage creativity and spontaneity. This is something I will not even debate. I have been there long enough to know it but frankly I realized all this only when I started to see all this happening with my son. In a bus, sit quietly because the driver will get disturbed; in a class, do not speak as the teacher will get disturbed. The climate is that of control. Everything in the class is directed towards taking an exam. The joy of learning is simply not there.

Subalaxmi further added,

I read somewhere in a school's prospectus—help your child climb the ladder of success. This sounds so funny and so immature. What does a three-year-old know about success? Do they even care about success that we in our narrow-minded vision have written for them and want them to believe as the gospel truth? A child simply wants to be happy. We want to be successful, we want to achieve, then why put the load of all this on the tiny shoulders of our kids? And for being successful, we set targets for them—learn alphabets by September, numbers by December and so on. Why are we doing this? And this is when we decided to pull him out of the school and homeschool him. Luckily, my husband also agreed and both of us are not very mainstream people either. This helped. Till now the homeschooling has worked very well or let me put it this way—far better than what a regular school would have done to my child.

I had started to see much better what Subalaxmi wanted to convey. But she did not stop there.

She went on saying,

Look at the typical schedule of a child. At 7 AM the bus comes to pick them up; most small kids are crying uncontrollably. They are stressed. Some of them are even puking in the bus. Most of their symptoms are psychosomatic. I can see the relief and satisfaction on the faces of parents when the bus leaves. It is like one more thing done from the list. For one more day I have been successful in sending my child to the school. But at what cost? Is the child happy? In the school, the learning is heavily structured, and one period follows the other. Small kindergarten kids are handed pencils and asked to write alphabets. The child does not even know what a pencil is! Let the child feel the pencil and explore it for a day. But no, we are in a hurry to make them literate. Another child, who has just found a way to solve a maths sum, is excited and wants to use the technique he has just learnt to solve the next sum. But just then the bell rings. The maths period is over and the English teacher has entered the class. This steamroller learning happens till afternoon and then the child returns home all tired, exhausted and with no desire to explore anything new. In the evening the child must do homework and then he is so tired that he goes off to sleep. Where is the time spent with parents? In those crucial childhood years, the time spent with the parents is so important for the child.

What Subalaxmi said is true. In most families these days, both parents are busy, and they prefer keeping the child in the school for longer if possible. In few cases that I came across, parents have admitted their children in schools that conduct special classes after normal schooling hours, to prepare them for admission to IITs, the premier engineering colleges in India. And this does not start from the 9th or 10th grade. This starts right from the primary grade. The kids remain in school till 4:30 in the evening and come back home only by dusk. Then the load of homework plus extra work is given in the special classes. One never finds such kids playing with other kids outdoors. But parents are happy and hopeful that their son will one day crack IIT entrance exam and change the course of his destiny.

Subalaxmi said,

We adults are anxiously searching for security. Most of the things we do are to create more and more security for ourselves. More so for our kids. In the process we are destroying their childhood, curiosity, imagination and the power to think and create. Not to forget, we are not raising a generation of happy kids.

An unhappy generation with an anxious, stressed mental state is a potential recipe for disaster as they approach adulthood.

A colleague once asked me what I was planning for my son. I told her that he is interested in a few things and is exploring them. Once he makes up his mind, then we will see. She made a very sharp comment at this stage that I will never forget: 'Yes, for the 85 per cent mass such an approach is fine, but if you want to be in the top 15 per cent then you need to plan carefully and do something different.' Mother of an eleven-year-old girl, she narrated how she has ensured that her daughter is among the toppers in the school and sent her to a summer school in the USA, where also she topped the group and is attending coaching classes to crack something 'big' in the future. Her daughter's achievements were praiseworthy and I wish her the very best in life, but I hope my colleague has ensured that her daughter is growing up to be a happy child. Interestingly though, I had found my colleague to be hypercompetitive to the extent that she will not hesitate to publicly scathe other colleagues to showcase her achievements. While her achievements were worth respect, I never found her to be exuding happiness. She was extremely neurotic, always on the edge, stressed, anxious and very critical and cynical about most of the things. Her physical health also seemed to be affected by her state of mind. If success comes at this cost, then is that really success?

Subalaxmi, who has taken a year-long sabbatical from her school to find a little more time for herself and for her son, added,

In the last one year we have spent so much quality time together. We have gone for morning forest treks or we have just sat under a tree and I have read out a poem to him explaining its meaning in the midst of nature. I can relate it with examples that he will connect better. As a mother I know what he likes most, and related examples work best to connect him with something, like a poetry. He reads, does experiments, learns from online videos and solves maths sums. There is no limit, no rigid structure for the same.

She also narrated how Akash got the opportunity to work in the prestigious NCBS labs at such a tender age:

Some people may question the lack of structure in his learning and doubt the knowledge that he has acquired. But on the contrary, that seems to have helped him a lot. We always used to take him for open days at IISc (Indian Institute of Science). When NCBS also started the concept of open days, we visited the research institute with Akash. During open days, the labs are open for general public; one can do experiments, interact with scientists, read about the work being done at the institute by the researchers and much more. At one such stall, Akash answered a lot of questions. At that time, a senior scientist, whom we later came to know as Professor Sumantra Chattarji, was passing by when one of his students quipped, 'Sir this boy is going to be your next scholar.' Professor Chattarji interacted with him and was very impressed by his knowledge. He was also fascinated by the fact that Akash was being homeschooled. He asked us to meet again. We met him, and he invited Akash to work in his lab. Later another scientist Dr Shashi also extended the invitation to Akash. He goes to NCBS labs twice a week for about two hours each day. The kind of exposure that Akash is having is unimaginable.

What about social behaviour? Is Akash learning that? Now as he approaches his higher grades, would he join a regular school? Would he have problems of fitting in in a system that might not be so flexible?

Subalaxmi said,

I do not claim to have all the answers, though I have most of them. In my opinion, both homeschooled and mainstream schooled children lose some and gain some. But the question is: What are they losing, and can it be fulfilled by other means? In the case of Akash, he goes to karate class, which is very structured and has clear rules that must be followed; then he plays a very rough sport called football. He sometimes gets bullied on the field. But now he is grown up enough for me to explain that the world will not always be fair to him, even though he would want them to be. Akash has now also overcome his fear of strict coach to learn swimming. I did not protect him there. In other words, Akash has learnt to be adaptable. Yes, like other main-stream school kids, he may not know how to push his way through, but that is fine. His competition is with himself and not with anyone else.

Indeed, Akash is very well-behaved and polite, a happy child with a wonderful sense of humour.

Would Akash have done better had he continued in a mainstream school? Anyone's guess!

In that case, are traditional mainstream schools losing their charm and significance? Do they understand the needs of this generation kids and facilitate learning? We see a mad rush for schools every year, parents scurrying for a seat in a prestigious school for their child, many a time to be greeted by snobbish admission managers who act pricey. In one case, that I know, the expecting parents started looking for a seat for their unborn child, as the most prestigious school in the city had three–four years waiting list for admission. Would all those parents after reading the story of Akash pull their kids out of the mainstream schools?

No, we do not expect such knee-jerk reactions. But the questions remain. Talking to countless parents, teachers, educationists and zeners themselves, I have been able to draw precious insights. And as an author, my job is to be unbiased in ensuring all such voices are heard equally, and together we can ensure that this generation of learners does not get a raw deal. We messed up to a large extent when it comes to millennials in their formative years but then that is beyond recall and repair. However, we still have an opportunity with the Gen Z kids and adolescents, and as parents, teachers, coaches and educators our responsibility cannot be more stressed upon and underlined.

Essentially, three kind of schooling beliefs exist these days— mainstream schooling, alternative schooling and homeschooling. Alternative schools do not believe in the teaching techniques that are used in mainstream schools and use a completely different approach in how they make the kids learn the lesson and lessons of life. These schools are few but have good footfalls. Majority of the schools fall in the category of mainstream schools. However, I have found that even within mainstream schools there are two subforms—the traditional mainstream schools and the modern mainstream schools. The former stress on rote learning, exams and grade. They offer very less room for any innovation. This is where the latter score. The modern mainstream schools allow innovation in teaching techniques to a large extent.

While Manaswati, a senior teacher and a social science expert, supports mainstream schooling, Deepa Raja, Principal Jnana Vikas Public School, Bengaluru, believes that all schooling techniques are unique, and parents should choose the schooling philosophy based on their child. However, both agree that whatever the type of schooling, teaching innovations with a focus only on learning makes all the difference.

The recent recommendations made by Government Textbook Society and Department of State Educational Research and Training (DSERT) regarding 'no homework, no books and no bag' policy have received mixed response from the society. These bodies recommend that school children should not be given any homework and there should be two 'no books and no school bag' days in a month. The idea is to release the children of the burden of learning. Most school managements have opposed the policy recommendations citing that this would stunt learning. In fact, they would rather treat no books, no bag days as holiday for kids to bond with family. In between all this cacophony, somewhere the cause of the children is getting lost all over again. Learning and leisure—can't we ensure these two basic privileges of kids? Learning cannot end in classrooms and heavy school bags and homework or no homework cannot ensure learning necessarily. It is funny that even when we have guidelines that the weight of a school bag should not be more than 10 per cent of the total weight of the child, kids continue to lunge to schools with bags weighing more than the permitted limit.

Class-Wise Weight Limit of School Bags Recommendations of HRD Ministry in India

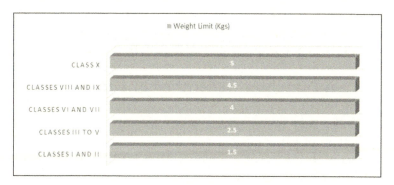

Source: The Hindu, available at https://www.thehindu.com/news/national/karnataka/karnataka-limits-weight-of-schoolbags/article27038764.ece/amp/ (accessed on 22 Nov 2019).

Even though the famous writer and novelist R. K. Narayan had raised the issue of heavy school bags in the Indian Parliament in the 1980s, and despite the fact that doctors have been repeatedly reminding that carrying heavy school bags can put undue stress on the muscles, ligaments and discs of kids, potentially damaging or weakening them, we have hardly done anything to address the issue. Civil society, government, lawmakers, policymakers, schools, teachers and parents, all must share the blame. We continue to plunge the kids into the juggernaut of education without really caring whether we can assure learning and at the same time ensure that kids have enough leisure time that allows them to think and ideate. UNICEF's Convention on the Rights of the Children (CRC) stipulates the right to rest and to engage in leisure activities. Schools in California have taken the most 'cost-effective' step to improve graduation rates among high schoolers. The lawmakers are recommending banning early-bird schools in California. No school will be able to start the classes before 8:30 AM. The recommendations that are being implemented for high-school as well as middle-school students are in line with findings that children who had longer time in bed were healthier and more likely to graduate. Research showed that teenagers especially benefited from sleeping later: lower depression and anxiety rates, higher attainment and fewer car accidents have all been associated with school starting times being pushed back in the USA.

A Different Generation of Learners

To understand how teaching needs to be facilitated to this generation of kids and adolescents, it is pertinent to understand them and their learning techniques. Most teachers get frustrated with the current lot of children primarily because they do not understand them and make the mistake of using old techniques and project their experiences on them. Zeners are a different generation of learners.

I See, I Do, I Learn

In an era of YouTube and abundance of visual content, the learning style of today's kids and adolescents has seen a continuity with the millennial generation. Learning styles refer to learning preferences of an individual, the way a person learns best. Visual learners learn best through images, videos, graphics and diagrams; auditory learners learn best through listening; while kinaesthetic or tactile learners learn best though activities or learning by doing. There may be a fourth category of learners who learn best using text (reading and writing). Most people are multimodal learners; that is, they learn using more than one mode, although they might have a dominant preference often referred to as learning styles. When teaching or training methods use tools and techniques commensurate with the learning style of the learners, learning is best facilitated. Research has shown that a generation or a population cohort has similar learning styles, since learning styles, like other attitudes, are shaped primarily by the environment. In my previous book, I had highlighted the learning style of millennials and multiple researches who have proved the same beyond doubt that they were primarily visual and kinaesthetic learners. Generation Z or zeners, as I call them, have inherited the same legacy of the millennials and they too have similar learning styles. A research by a premier generational research agency in Australia, McCrindle Foundation, shows that zeners are visual and kinaesthetic learners. In very simple words, they learn best using the visual medium and/ or learning by doing, that is, through activity-based learning. Manisha Kumari, who works as a teacher, says 'This generation of kids wants practical hands-on experience. They will not just believe hearsay. They want to do it and try it before believing it.'

Technology Wizards

Zeners take to technology like a fish takes to water. If millennials were inundated with technology when they were growing up, then zeners have been born in the cradle of technology. You do not have to teach them technology. They just learn it organically as if they knew it before even it was invented. When I call them technology wizards, it does not mean in terms of operating gadgets or smartphones. This is the simpler part. I have seen young boys and girls talking about advanced technological innovations. When Arnab wanted to attend the Google I/O machine learning meetup organized by the Google Developers Group (GDG), Bahrain, I was not sure if they would allow him to attend. When I chatted with the organizers they welcomed him with open arms. We decided to take Arnab for the meetup thinking it would be a good exposure for him and motivate him. However, as the youngest member to attend the meet, he drew attention with his sharp answers and ideas. To our surprise, complete strangers came to us and told us great things about our son. I do not know how far this would really continue, but I must confess that despite being very much in sync with what his interests are, I was surprised by his knowledge about technology. And I am sure that Arnab is not the only young tech wizard. This is a generation that is flying on the wings of technology.

Social Learners

Social media plays a big role in the way they learn. Social media enables them to learn from the larger environment. It also helps connect to a huge network and learn from each other. Zeners are the first generation to imbibe social learning in the truest sense, since they are getting exposed to the same in their formative years.

MOOCs Learners

Massive open online courses or MOOCs are heralded as a revolution in the field of education. Millennials were the first generation to be exposed to these, and now zeners are getting exposed to the same from an early age. MOOCs enable the remote reach of universities and other skill-imparting institutions to students all over the world. MOOC platforms such as Coursera, Udemy, edX, Alison and many more are drawing millions of students all over the world. MOOCs offer zeners an opportunity to learn skills relevant for them in the future from an early age. When I see my son interested in learning Python basics for artificial intelligence (AI) from a similar platform DataCamp, I know this is touching many of his age as well. The course is offered free of cost.

Explorers

Zeners are explorers. They love to explore possibilities, beyond the obvious. The obvious is many a time dictated by the parents, teachers and other elders around, drawing lines of possibilities. However, this generation considers possibilities as limitless. They want to explore what they learn and learn through exploration. They question the validity of studying anything that will not help them in the future.

Global yet Local Distractions

Zeners are global citizens. They are well connected online and most of them have travelled, which has given them a wide-angle exposure to the world that we live in. Daisy Bastian, Head of the Department (Languages and Social Sciences for CAIE and ICSE/ISC) at Deccan International School, says,

Today's classrooms are culturally, linguistically and ethnically far more diverse than it had been a decade ago. Majority of them live in cosmopolitan societies, have travelled more and bring in a global perspective. Still they find it difficult at times to create inclusive relationships in classrooms, as even as kids they imbibe strong feelings for cultural and traditional misconceptions.

She goes on to exemplify how she has witnessed 2nd grade students arguing and fighting over the other child's choice of food and food habits. She goes on to add, 'Society is mirrored in the classrooms. By and large, they lack skills in interpersonal relationships.'

Assertive

'Zeners are extremely assertive to the extent of becoming argumentative at times', says Manaswati, 'They are not the ones who can be easily convinced and persuaded.' In many ways, this is true. They are highly informed and cannot be convinced otherwise, unless one has a logical evidence to make them believe so. Manaswati adds,

They are not afraid to speak their mind. You are dealing with hard nuts in the class and only the competent teacher gets respected. You just cannot demand respect anymore because of your position. Poor teachers can no longer manage the class with the power of the stick.

Curious Learners

Zeners have a lot of questions, and they also have a lot to opine and share. 'Every child knows how to attract attention. If you do not let them answer or let them ask their questions, they will do something not so constructive to attract your attention', says Manaswati from her teaching experience. Their learning experiences need to be more engaged. A traditional lecture method will not capture their attention and satisfy their curiosity.

Goal-oriented Learners Who Expect Quick Results

'As learners, they are goal oriented—they want to be sportsmen, musicians, fashion designers, dancers, artists, etc., and have interests outside their classrooms. They are self-confident and knowledge-able', feels Daisy Bastian. She further adds,

However, they expect quick results and success and are easily discouraged and can give up on their dreams if there are no support systems to sustain their goals. Emotional support and acceptance of their uniqueness are expected by every learner of this generation. They learn only if learning is fun and they feel happy! As educators, we need to be well equipped to provide them with an array of learning tools and techniques to build relationships.

Sage on the Stage or Facilitator on the Sidelines?

The era when teachers used to be 'sage on the stage' and whatever they utter used to be accepted as the gospel truth is gone. Deepa Raja, a senior academic, says,

This generation of kids is different. They know what they want and what they don't. They use a lot of technology and are very aware of things around them. They have high clarity of what they want and start taking their decisions very early. Hence, parents and teachers need to be more like facilitators, where they guide and channelize the energies of the children, rather than dictate terms to them. When we were kids, we used to be more like followers. It used to come to a stage where even after growing up we would still want our parents to support us and then our parents would tell us the importance of being on our own. Because of this, many a time we would make choices based on our parent's instructions and later realize that that was not what we wanted to do. Generally, it would be too late by the time we realize that. This is not how the current generation processes information these days. They do not easily follow instructions. They are much more independent and clearer in their heads. A baggage that comes with this independence is that they are perhaps not as respectful towards elders as we used to be when we were kids. But all said and done, our role has changed to that of a facilitator.

Deepa is correct in her assessment. It is pertinent to remember that we are dealing with a different generation of learners who no more need to go to schools to acquire knowledge and infor-mation. They get plenty and more through the World Wide Web and social media. They need to go to school for learning and for knowing how to apply them in the real world. This alters the role of teachers and schools completely. They no more can remain as information and knowledge disseminators. They must instead take up the role of learning facilitators. Their words will not be accepted by the students as the gospel truth; instead, they would be scrutinized based on their ability to create an environment of learning and ensure that learning can be facilitated and accelerated.

At a time when online tuitions and private tutors are flourishing, the role of teachers needs a lot of introspection and the whole gamut of teaching needs transformation. Private tutors, coaching classes, online coaching, all are flourishing. Take BYJU's, the online tuitions for schools students, for instance. With its mammoth $540-million funding at a valuation of $3.6 billion, BYJU's has entered the top tier of the club of Indian unicorns—start-ups valued at $1 billion and over—becoming the fourth-most-valued start-up in the country. In future, it also has plans to go public with an IPO. What makes these companies so profitable? There must be something lacking in schools that makes BYJU's or companies like them so profitable. The findings of the *Cambridge International Global Education Census Report* show that Indian school students take the maximum tutorial lessons. Nearly 74 per cent of the students take tutorial lessons in mathematics. The study also found out lower involvement of school students in extra-curricular activities, sports and even free play activities. Only 3 per cent school students in India play more than six hours a week. The report terms the life of school children in India as 'hectic'. This is a global study that involves other countries of the world as well and does not augur well for the future.

Sourabh Kumar, who is a private tutor himself, says, 'Students whom I teach are hesitant in asking questions in schools for the fear of being mocked at. However, they ask a lot of questions during tuition classes.' He blames this on crass commercialization of education and lack of accountability of academic institutions in assurance of learning. He says,

Most schools and teachers do not bother whether students learn or not. Teachers are more focused on finishing course syllabus and not on clearing doubts of students. When you do not listen to the students they lose interest. One-way communication will never work with this current generation of learners.

It is quite a strong and frank comment on the schooling system. He adds,

The education system and the whole process of teaching need to change. The current generation of learners question the utility of whatever they study. Once one of my students asked me how the principle of probability gets practically applied in our day-to-day lives. Frankly, I did not have an immediate answer. I had to do a bit of research and answer his question. Do most teachers have that kind of patience, time and knowledge these days?

Deepa says,

Teachers are bound by lesson plans in school. The target right from the beginning of the academic session is to finish the syllabus. If a teacher goes to the class with that kind of mindset, then they are sure to mess up. The unfulfilled need of the student in the class is fulfilled by online tuitions and private tutors.

Rachana Bhawsar, a senior teacher with a school, says, 'I cannot go beyond the syllabus. Otherwise, I will keep teaching the same chapter or topic for a long time. I can go beyond syllabus once I complete the same.'

We often find schools or teachers blaming the central education boards for being restrictive, binding them with rules or policies that do not allow free thinking and learning through experiences. Rachana who has had an opportunity to work closely with the Central Board of Secondary Education (CBSE) differs. She goes on to outline how CBSE has evolved and has reinvented itself.

She further adds that most parents do not care to check out the facts before blaming, and schools implement the recommendations based on their will and intent. The good ones implement in letter and spirit the innovations in curriculum, while others just play to the gallery and ensure paper compliance. Rachana implores parents to cross-check the facts before blaming the board and at the same time hold schools more accountable. Rachana is not alone in her defence for the central board in India. Manisha Kumari and few other teachers like her spoke about how CBSE has tried to keep pace with the changing learning needs of this generation. Rachana exemplifies the Continuous and Comprehensive Evaluation (CCE), a scheme of CBSE that has inbuilt flexibility for schools to plan their own academic schedules as per specified guidelines on CCE. Problem Solving Assessment (PSA) is yet another different measure to create an enjoyable learning environment and stimulate curiosity and creativity among kids. It has been designed to improve the generic and higher-order thinking skills.

Daisy Bastian, a senior academic herself, who has been on both sides of the fences, as a teacher as well as an administrator, says

Today every board has evolved and urges teachers to be innovative. Having worked in CBSE, ICSE, IGCSE and IB curriculum, I can say with conviction that every teacher has the freedom to engage students creatively in his/her classroom. However, it does take good deal of planning to make a lesson engaging and fun. Resources could be a problem in certain situations, but no one can stop your creativity.

One then wonders that if the central board is introducing innovations in curriculum, then why by and large it appears that the teaching institutions have not been able to keep pace with the changing generational needs and expectations!

Implementation on ground is as important as innovating in terms of policies. It is important to ensure execution of those policies. Schools and teachers need to be sensitized and equipped for the same. Further innovations cannot be unidimensional in nature. Lesson plans need to be flexible and take into consideration the different needs of every child. Teaching needs to use innovative techniques for a generation that no longer comes to school for knowledge. They come to learn, and teachers will do a great job facilitating the same. Curricular innovations are not enough without understanding how the whole gamut of learning needs to change. The shift needs to happen from conventional learning to experiential learning that can provide meaningful experiences to the zeners. Experiential learning uses multiple intelligences that enhances students' comprehension and reinforces content through active participation. Teachers need to be facilitators, guiding the student to master the content with the scaffolding techniques that encourage them to think independently, critically and creatively. At the same time, technology needs to be integrated that further becomes an enabler in the process of learning.

Deepa visualizes her role as a facilitator. She says,

As a teacher, I am a facilitator of learning. I first need to know what my students know and then help them to know it better. I help them recall their life experiences and apply the same to learning new concepts in the class. Then I use their new learning to help them understand how to apply it in their day-to-day lives.

Daisy Bastian adds,

I have been fortunate enough to work in schools where teachers' role as facilitators had been acknowledged. Many teachers utilize audio–video tools and real-life learning methods (through field trips) to teach concepts. KWL charts, brainstorming for ideas or to assess what is already known, mind-mapping, etc., are increasingly used in the classrooms. Students and teachers are encouraged to present concepts/ideas through graphic organizers. Role-playing is a technique that I have used extensively to give insights into real-life situations. Introducing history lessons like a story is one of the techniques used by a colleague of mine who made history memorable in the classroom.

The Outside-In Approach

Deepa Raja, principal of a well-known school, has made her way to the top post primarily because of her different outlook towards the new generation of learners and for her teaching innovations. In her present role, she is perfectly poised to guide other teachers into nurturing the zeners better. She remarks,

Every child is unique, more so for this new generation who are independent and informed. As a teacher I have always found that it is difficult to teach using only lesson plans. At times the children do not relate to the examples mentioned in the lesson plan. Teaching is about understanding those unique needs and responding to the same.

Deepa Raja narrates an instance. While teaching grammar in her class, the lesson plan demanded an activity to be done in the class to teach noun to the kids. However, instead of using flash cards or the other more routine ones, Deepa used a different technique altogether. She asked kids to find objects around them (common noun). Then she asked them to note the person next to them (proper noun). Through the act of visualization, she urged them to recall the things and people they encountered while commuting from home to school. After a while, the kids started to see nouns all around them. They could relate far better. No flash cards or lecture could help them do that so easily. She used the same approach to teach shapes in mathematics to the primary kids. In that week, she discussed with and requested all other teachers teaching the class to use that shape in their lessons somehow. For instance, when square was being taught, then the drawing teacher would make them draw various square things in the art class. Even parents were urged to send sandwiches as tiffin without slicing the bread. The kids saw that what they were eating was also a square.

Manaswati, someone who is known for her innovative teaching techniques, winner of teaching awards such as the Sincere Teacher Award and the Science Olympiad Foundation International Award and greatly respected in the academic circles, adds,

Whenever I have to teach a lesson in social science, I ask them to identify the main words in that chapter. Then I ask them to find words similar to those key words or any incident around those words. For instance, say the key word is mountain; they can tell me words that are synonyms of mountains, even in their own language or they can share their stories about mountains, say the last time they went on a holiday to a hill station. This helps them to understand the central theme of the chapter so well that it becomes almost a cake walk for them to learn the chapter, not to talk about the keen interest with which they learn afterwards.

Sanchita, who teaches economics and global perspectives to senior grade students at Akash International School, stresses upon the need to connect the lessons with the real-life examples.

Bookish examples do not work much. They must connect what they are learning with what's happening in real life. While teaching the concept of price elasticity of demand, I gave the examples of

how price of school uniforms increase just before the beginning of the academic session and how it impacts the parent's pockets, why the tickets for the qualifiers of world cup are priced lower as compared to the finals or semi-finals of the world cup as the demand for them becomes inelastic at that time and, for that matter, flight tickets bought at the last moment are costlier than what we buy one month before our travel.

She further illustrates,

One day while teaching social prejudices and biased behaviour based on caste in civics, I asked one student in my class if she has experienced anything similar. She told the class how she has witnessed some families use different utensils for serving people of other religions and they are being washed with a different detergent soap and kept separate from the other household utensils.

The Inside-Out Approach

Deepa Raja, who besides her role as a senior academic also has been a parent counsellor, seems to be stressing on the need to build on the experiences of the kids and using those to not only teach them a lesson but also help them understand how to apply that learning in their day-to-day lives. She continues with her grammar example. Once the kids finished the chapter on nouns, the next chapter to be taught to them was on adjectives. Now that they had identified things and people around them, they were asked to note down their positive and negative qualities. Deepa, who connects teaching to daily experiences of the kids, adds, 'Teaching adjectives in this manner made them realize that every person has god qualities and area of improvement. No one is perfect, but we need to accept them the way they are and then try to change them for good.' Deepa recalls the time when she was teaching in a school that was in Jalgaon, Maharashtra, one of the hottest places in India. During summers, the temperature would soar to 45 °C–46 °C. Deepa adds,

The kids would feel warm and irritated to come to school. But when they learnt the above lesson, I made them do a follow-up exercise where they wrote down the positive and negative things about summer season. They learnt that instead of complaining if we accept life and the good and not-so-pleasant things that come together, then it becomes much easier. The kids in my class were far happier, much less irritated during the entire summer. Somewhere their attitudes had been shaped.

Deepa shares another example. After teaching them basic operation in mathematics such as addition and subtraction, she gave the kids an exercise to keep an account of their own expenses. This small activity made them realize their expenditure and savings on their pocket money. Most of them started managing their pocket money better instead of spending everything very soon.

In another such example, Deepa shares how she teaches her students the importance of having backup plans in life when she teaches about planning. Deepa adds,

I always tell them to have three plans, Plans A, B and C. If Plan A does not work, then Plan B will, and if Plan B doesn't, then at least Plan C will work. This helps them to do the same in their lives. They do not get depressed if things do not work out initially for them. Instead with backup plans they become more and more resilient and prepared to face failures or disappointments.

Sanchita adds,

Once in an economics workshop while teaching international trade, I made the students represent different countries selling one item each, followed by a small skit to help them understand how international trade works on comparative advantage by showcasing what a country would produce and what it would import based on least opportunity cost. It worked well, and students were able to understand the topic in a better way. Thereafter it was not only easy for them to understand the complex graph of comparative advantage, but they also understood the practical application of economic theories in international trade.

Visual Induction

Parmesh is a 4th grade student. Manaswati is his class teacher. It is not easy to gain and retain Parmesh's attention. He is a restless bundle of energy. Although very sweet and a darling of his teachers, when it comes to teaching him it is no child's play. He does not write properly and during lectures he sifts through other things. Manaswati says,

You have to see what happens once I play a video related to the lesson in the class. Parmesh just transforms. One who is restless during other times is just glued to the screen. He is so hooked by the video that you cannot divert his attention. And after the video, Parmesh is the first student to explain the same.

I call this the visual induction effect. Manaswati says that it's the same with other kids when it comes to being hooked to visual content. However, video is not the only visual content that she uses in the class. She uses various props at times in the class to create a visual content. She exemplifies,

I had to teach a chapter on water. The day when that chapter was scheduled, I placed a glass of water on my table in the class. Kids invariably ask questions whenever they find something unusual or out of place. Even before we started reading the chapter, they learnt that water is colourless, it takes the shape of the container that it is placed in and many other properties of water. An impromptu discussion triggered by the glass of water that I had placed on the table. The idea was to make them curious and let questions come from them, rather than me asking them questions.

Get In On the Act

Zeners also learn by doing. Activity-based learning has been advocated since quite some time; however, there could not be a better time when this needs to be implemented. While many teachers struggle to fit in activities where schools do not encourage such forms of learning or are cowed by the pressure of syllabi, Manaswati has innovated a unique activity that she calls 'circle time'.

Circle Time

Manaswati says, 'Activities need not to be built only in the lessons. There are many ways to innovate on activities and ensure that kids are involved and engaged even before the learning starts.' As a class teacher of a primary section, she has innovated an activity that she calls circle time. She ensures that she reaches her class a bit early in the morning.

Kids start coming into the class. The time before the bell rings for the assembly and prayer, Manaswati gets together the kids who have arrived early. She holds hands with kids and makes them go round in circles. After a couple of rounds, they sit in a circle formation on the ground. Then each kid can share whatever they want to—they might sing a song, recite a poem, tell about a newspaper headline or tell about some experience. This activity allows free flow of expressions and energizes the kids before the class begins. They become de-stressed, alert and happy for the class. A good start to the day can accelerate and elevate learning experiences. The kids in fact compete against each other to find a place next to Manaswati when they sit in a circle.

However, this is not the only way Manaswati involves her students in activities. She uses innovative activity-based learning and her techniques are unique yet simple, therefore exemplary.

Manaswati was teaching the chapter on adaptation. She encouraged kids to use various waste material, twigs and leaves to make nests in the class. One such nest she kept on the table in the veranda adjoining the classroom. Two days later, they found out that a bird had laid eggs in that nest, mistaking it for a real one. Manaswati says,

The kids were overjoyed with excitement. They were witnessing their chapter coming to life. The whole experience became so real that it generated a lot of curiosity and interest among kids. Do you have to tell them to learn the chapter after that? They just do it on their own.

In another class, when she was teaching a chapter on air, she encouraged kids to make paper planes and fans. She says, 'Initially the kids did not believe their ears. Their teacher was asking them to make paper planes and fly them in the class. Luckily our school allows such activities to engage the kids. They were so excited, and they learnt everything in play.' Some nice paper planes and fans were displayed on the board by Manaswati and she says, 'Kids understood so easily that something that they cannot touch or see called air is so important in their day-to-day lives.'

Stay and Stray

Daisy shares an effective method that she has been using very successfully which she calls as 'stay and stray'. Stay and stray is a gallery walk-through of the student group presentations displayed by them on charts. Prior to the preparation of the charts, the students in groups go through the resources and present the required content asked by the teacher. Each group is given a different topic. All these charts are displayed in a gallery. Turn by turn, one of the groups stays back for presentation at their assigned spot in the gallery, while other groups take a gallery walk. Everyone gets a chance to present the content and listen to the presentations as well.

Daisy Bastian adds,

Students like to interact; they value friendship with peers and teachers and if learning can happen through these social interactions that would be ideal. Hence, I make use of this as a teacher and encourage other teachers to use the same. Think–pair–share, group discussions, peer interaction, debates, sharing of thoughts, learning games, etc., are good ways to get them socially engaged in the classroom.

Comfortable reading and study areas, play time, freedom to move around or sit anywhere in the class, raise questions and air opinions help in the learning process. The brain is stimulated during physical activities, and I have used it well in planning my classes.

Storytelling

Storytelling works in a big way in engaging these kids in the process of learning. Manaswati uses stories extensively in her teaching. She informs,

I was teaching mass communication to my students. Lots of pigeons come to our school every day. I spun the story around the pigeons. I told them how in olden days, pigeons were used to relay messages afar and how message notes used to be tied to their feet and they would fly long distances to deliver the message to the intended recipient. From there I took them to the advent of post office and later to the evolution of telephones, telegrams and then to modern Internet-based digital communication and media communication. You could see the amazement on their faces. They live in a completely different era and it is hard for them to believe that pigeons indeed relayed messages. When I was teaching another set of kids a chapter on Buddhism and Jainism, I told them how these sects believe in complete non-violence to the extent that they would not even harm a microbe throughout their physical existence. I told them a story about my childhood, when I had gone to South India as a tourist. I saw one person walking with a broom in his hands. He was incessantly sweeping the floor before him before stepping on that piece of ground. I had asked my father the logic of doing this as it seemed quite painful for the person who had to do it. That is when my father told me about these religions and the belief behind such acts. When the kids heard this story, they told me how they had seen few Jain people wearing white face masks or ensuring that they eat only before sunrise or after sunset so as not to harm any insect even unknowingly. They contribute so much to the class and their learning is accelerated.

But storytelling need not be done only by the teachers. Daisy Bastian seems to build on the success stories of the zeners in her class and uses well the fact that most zeners are achievers and have something or the other to share about their success and their journey. She says,

One of the techniques I have used in the classroom to motivate and guide students is facilitating sharing of success stories. All achievers in my classroom, be it in sports, arts, theatre, music, dance or academics, have a chance to share how they have prepared themselves for the event and what they thought helped them achieve what they have achieved. The rest of the class could interview the winner. This helps them learn that extraordinary achievements come with focus, grit and consistent work.

Choice-based Credits

Choice-based credits are prevalent in higher education in top-rung universities where students can choose courses based on their choice from a basket of courses. This allows varied learning paths for students while taking up the same programme as per their interests and aptitude. Choice-based credits are unheard in schools. But why do we expect every child to have a similar learning path? We talk about multiple intelligences in our research papers and talks at international forums and seminars, yet when it comes to ground-level implementation we neither show intent nor an urgency to do the same. Amrutha, a teenager who has just appeared for 10th grade board exams, wants to pursue legal studies after her schooling. She wonders why she can't study law as an optional course in the last two years of her schooling. She must compulsorily choose science, arts or commerce stream. She says,

I know that most of what I am going to study will not be of any use to me after I pass out in next two years, yet I will have to go through this process. I would have been much better enriched if I could choose a foundational basic course of legal aspects.

Ravi, a student in the 8th grade, wants to be a musician when he grows up; Keerthan wants to be a data scientist; and Tanya wants to be an animator. Choice-based credits are the need of the hour, and some degree of flexibility needs to be built in the curriculum to allow students choose their learning paths, rather than trying to brand them as only science students, arts students or commerce students. Will it be easy to implement? Definitely not! But then any change is difficult in the beginning, especially transformational changes. But when we look at the benefits, they far outweigh the cost in terms of time, energy and resources needed to integrate choice-based credits.

Industry–School Partnerships

We talk about industry–academia partnerships in higher education, why not right from schools? After all, these are the foundation and formative years when kids must be exposed to what the industry is working on, the kind of technologies and innovations that are being practised and planned, and what the future is likely to be. A visit to a start-up incubation centre, for instance, can open the world of possibilities to the zeners. Considering that zeners are highly informative, understand technology really well and are extremely creative, such early exposures can be a tipping point for this entire generation and for the world at large.

Open Book Exams

In a first of its kind, a school in Mysore (India) conducted open book exams for children from 5th to 10th grades. The school held closed book and open book tests for the same subjects on consecutive days. The teachers reported that students were more relaxed inside the examination hall as well as after coming out of the examination hall after finishing the open book test. The school also reported positive feedback from students regarding the open book exams. The school deserves accolades for experimenting with the innovative idea based on the recommendations of the state education minister. Open book exams have the potential of not only easing the examination phobia and stress among children but also considerably revolutionizing the way teaching–learning occurs and the way students are evaluated. Most of the present exams are memory tests that have little room for application-based questioning. This in turn means that teaching in classrooms is also centred around only conceptual learning and ensuring that students have theoretical knowledge. By contrast, open book exams have put an end to the memory test and moved closer towards application-based questions where students are not expected to memorize the concepts; instead, they learn how to apply them in real life. This naturally will change the whole landscape of teaching–learning. The teachers can no longer focus on teaching concepts and theories; they will have to focus on application.

Gamification

Gamification is not very new to learning scenarios. In simple words, gamification is the process of introducing game elements in non-game and non-leisure situations. When a classroom integrates the use of some of these elements, then the environment can be considered 'gamified'. Gamification of learning has been there for some time. But its application in school education is very recent and is challenging the traditional form of the teaching–learning process. Gamification is an approach of education that helps students learn to use video games and game elements in learning contexts. The objective is to capture the interest and attention of the new-age learners and ensure maximum enjoyment and engagement.

One common complaint that most parents have about their kids is that they are constantly on their phones playing games. Gamification in learning can exploit this behaviour of zeners positively and ensure that they learn to use games with greater responsibility for their development while they also have fun.

One such company gamifying the landscape of school education is PlayAblo. The company which cites its vision as 'taking the boring out of learning' and mission as 'to bring meaningful and engaging learning to masses, leveraging human-assistive technologies that are scalable and affordable' has won several awards for its PlayAblo gaming app. PlayAblo has won the EdTechReview Award: Game Based Learning Company of the Year (2019) and before that it won the EdTechReview Award: Skill Development Company of the Year (2018).

I decided to speak to two of the founders of this company, to understand how they are integrating gamification to school education through their application. Romal Bhulani, VP—Product Advisory, says,

At the heart of any successful learning experience lies the age-old adage, 'Practice makes perfect.' However, with the metamorphosis of the human computer interfacing and the proliferation of mobile Internet over the last decade, the learners today are faced with an environment that is extremely distracting, to say the least. Traditional methods of practising, paper-based worksheets, have rapidly lost favour and with that has come the decline of the learners' interest for in-depth understanding of their subjects. This is not to say that the learners from this age onwards will no longer be adept at any skill. It is just that the mechanism that will get them to practise will need to evolve and leverage the medium they prefer. This is where gamification fits in. It is important to note that gamification does not mean a video game. Gamification converts the erstwhile boring chores into an experience that resembles the benefits of playing a game, namely points, badges and leader boards (with their friends on it).

So how is gamification changing the learning landscape in schools? Romal adds,

Making exercises and assignments more fun is an obvious usage. It can also be used to track and reward the students reviewing additional resources referred by their teacher, and teachers getting rewarded for their overall class performance and effective coverage of their portions and identifying the best practices when tracking the outcomes from multiple classes across school branches. Gamification makes the entire education system at the school transition quick, from monotonous to motivated. And that will make all the difference.

The company has been trying to use the PlayAblo app to integrate gamification to learning. They collaborate with curriculum teams of schools to customize their content to suit the gamified experience and build automated insightful reports. Dheeraj Sharma, co-founder of PlayAblo, adds,

By customization we literally mean that we map our gamified assessment 100 per cent to the individual school's lesson plan. The teachers can give assignments on the exact small topic that they covered in the class and get feedback on the spot or within a day (if they give a homework assignment). This experience motivates not only the learners but also the trainers and teachers with actionable insights that they can use to improve the learning outcomes.

Dheeraj claims that the PlayAblo gamification app is a win-win proposition for students, teachers and schools alike. For students, it offers a fun-learning experience through the gamified platform encouraging intrinsic motivation for the learners. It provides strong conceptual grounding through structured learning built on top of the globally recognized Webb's Depth of Knowledge (DoK) framework. The framework sets the environment to help students move from lower-order thinking skills to higher-order thinking skills. For this purpose, the content is mapped to the Webb's DoK foundational framework (recall–concept–analytical–synthesis). As far as teachers are concerned, it offers an app or browser-based assessment platform that serves as a granular dashboard providing individual student-specific progress cards with customized learning recommendations. It helps save up to 40 hours per month for every teacher with the paperwork and effort surrounding student assessment. And since each PlayAblo implementation is custom configured in terms of the content alignment for the institution's curriculum/lesson plan, it allows PlayAblo to be used effectively as an in-curriculum tool. The school management also stands to gain from the implementation as it improves teacher productivity. It also helps them easily identify best practices across various learning centres and create a dashboard that highlights relative performances of different branches/sections.

So, can gamification completely replace traditional school pedagogy? Romal says,

Yes, but for most schools the jump is too drastic and the education system in India (as well as globally) is infamous for being painfully slow to transform. So to begin with, gamification will work best being complimentary, working hand in hand with the existing process, eliminating the manual and mechanical work of the teacher, allowing her more time at hand while dramatically increasing student involvement and participation.

Interestingly though, there is an extreme example also available— a school that runs entirely on the concept of gamification and has results to back its approach. Quest to Learn, a New York-based middle and high school, is a school that has its entire pedagogy built on the framework of gamification. Quest to Learn is a public 6–12 school with an innovative educational philosophy developed by top educators and game theorists at the Institute of Play, with funding from the MacArthur Foundation.

Is gamification the future of school education? Perhaps yes, in many ways. But the future belongs to innovative technologies and innovative teaching methods that are designed based on our right understanding of a new generation of learners. Only then we will be able to cater to their needs and ensure that our schools start creating minds and souls which are liberated from the shackles of mediocrity.

Dheeraj and Romal sign off by saying,

First and foremost, we (ed-tech innovators) need to realize that no one alone will have a silver bullet to solve all the problems currently faced by the education system. There will need to be a strong collaborative effort from multiple players that must include the school itself to make the leap. We anticipate that in the not-too-distant future, other than gamification other innovations will play a big role in education like use of augmented/virtual reality-based learning solutions, AI- and ML-driven self-adapting learning to personalize the learning for individual students and voice-based interactive solutions. Alexa and Google Home are just the tip of the iceberg. These will evolve significantly over the next three–five years to take the learning experience to a whole different level.

Are our schools, teachers and parents ready for this shift?

Role Reorientation

Besides being a facilitator of learning, teachers need to reorient their roles while dealing with a generation that is high in potential, knowledgeable, informed, creative and surer of what they want to do but at times besotted with unique life issues that we have never experienced in our childhood. Daisy Bastian feels,

Teachers no longer are a source of all knowledge. Skill sets for learning to learn and live, managing emotions and relationships, and grooming in empathy and compassion through right exposure and guidance are what a student requires from schools and teachers. The content-based curriculum should give way for the skill- and attitude-based curriculum where skills to learn and an ability to decide what to learn and how much to learn should be imparted to students. As a teacher, one needs to be empathetic and compassionate, and help students gain skills in problem-solving, critical thinking and creative thinking. Students must learn how to take care of oneself and manage daily life. Besides imparting participation skills to them, they should be taught about getting involved and building a sustainable future. Help should be extended to make them self-aware and good communicators.

Using the content that one teaches, one needs to impart these skills and universal values by modelling them for life. A teacher's job is very challenging and demanding in today's world but highly rewarding as well.

Friend, Philosopher, Guide

A teacher and a student can never be friends is what most people would think, perhaps. And, hence, advocating teachers to become friends of their students might be unacceptable to many. However, before you jump to a conclusion, it is pertinent to remember the changed group of learners and learning context. The new generation learners or our very own zeners would listen to a friend rather than follow an order. Besides, the learning context is changing or needs to change from one that believes in plain dissemination of knowledge to one that bridges the learning gap. Daisy Bastian very aptly remarks, 'Learning can be facilitated through an in-depth understanding of the learner through building trust-based relationships with the students and knowing his or her aptitudes.'

Being friend to the students means creating an environment of trust, a secure zone where zeners feel happy to share, differ (from the teacher) and ask (questions). Manaswati says,

I have at times done jogging with my students during their sports period or in a substitution period given them the opportunity of free expression (dance, song, storytelling) or with more senior students discussed about life. They have become so open that they have started sharing about what's going on in their lives. Some of them have even shared about their boyfriends and girlfriends. This helps them to relax and feel open to share. Some might think that when I do all this and become their friend, they will stop respecting me. But we are living in an age when respect comes from your competency in helping and guiding them through their problems rather by position. For my students, I am their friend, philosopher and guide.

Same sentiments are echoed by Daisy Bastian, however in a slightly different context. She says,

Today, we find a lot more students with stress symptoms as they have tight schedules and they lack skills for time management, resulting in burnout. Student expectations on grades have gone up, and there is a high level of competition and higher cut-off percentages, compelling them to work to meet those expectations from the society. Hence, every teacher needs to enable her/his students to be grounded, set realistic expectations from oneself and impart skills of time management. I was teaching the 10th grade and my learners were at different levels of performance. A few of them were below average when it came to analysis and application of their knowledge. The students were highly stressed with tuitions, unable to comprehend concepts and apply them, which added to the anxiety of impending board exams. When I sat with them individually, I helped them articulate their concerns and strategize their daily micro time management of study schedules. My experiential knowledge that learning can be impacted by diet, exercise and stress helped guide the students. As the adage goes, I think a teacher is a friend, philosopher and guide.

Teaching with Passion

Teaching is not among the most-respected and highest-paid jobs in most countries including India. This is the bitter truth. And that is one of the major reasons why our country lacks quality teachers who can bring innovations in classroom and make learning a joyful experience. Recently, the Centre for Teacher Accreditation (CENTA), Bengaluru conducted an Olympiad for teachers based on Teaching Professionals' Olympiad (TPO), an event that is organized every year. The performance of teachers in the Olympiad (2017) in which nearly 8,000 teachers participated from across the country was abysmal. Nearly 50 per cent of the teachers recorded a below average score of 35 per cent. The score was poor on three parameters: classroom practices and professional competencies (38%), logical abilities and communication (47%) and subject expertise (35%). This is a vicious cycle that refuses to be broken until fundamental reforms are affected in selection and hiring of teachers and revamping their compensation. The number of poor and average teachers outnumber the good teachers, and when such teachers go to classrooms, they cannot be expected to understand the new generation of learners and bring innovations in their teaching. A Comptroller Auditor General (CAG) report also revealed that close to 90 per cent of the teachers in special education lack qualification in both government and voluntary organization-run schools.

Deepa Raja, a senior academic and principal, says,

Teaching needs passion. Many people get into teaching because it pays decently, demands lesser working hours compared to corporate and has more vacations. These are wrong reasons to take up teaching as a profession. A teacher is like the mother of the class. Once you accept that, then your whole attitude changes and you do for your students like you will for your own child.

Views of Rachana Bhawsar are no different than of Deepa. She adds,

Good teachers join tuition classes as they get good money. The schools have very few quality teachers. I have myself seen women who join teaching for some extra pocket money or untrained teachers with no background in teaching joining schools. Many schools are also happy as they get them cheap. Such teachers will never be able to deliver.

Early experiences of the childhood play a major role in shaping attitudes in the future. Take for instance a research study reported in the *Translational Journal of the American College of Sports Medicine*. It found correlation between negative childhood experiences in physical education classes and attitudes towards physical activity later in adult life. Those who had negative childhood experiences in physical education like 'feeling embarrassed' or 'lack of enjoyment' displayed lack of enthusiasm towards physical activity in their adult life. They also spent considerably less time in gym or in other physical activities. While, on the contrary, those who had positive childhood experiences in physical education like 'receiving positive recognition from peers or teachers regarding their performance or action' showed greater liking towards physical activity in their adult life, spending considerably more time in gym or in other physical activities. If this can happen for physical education classes in school, it will be only safe to assume that there exists a strong relationship between other childhood experiences in which school classes, as a major portion, play a significant role in shaping most of their attitudes towards various elements of life later in their adult life. You must have found a lot many adults not liking mathematics. Most likely they have been 'terrorized' about this subject in their childhood. They would have had a horrible teacher of mathematics in their school when they were kids who gave an impression that learning maths was a rocket science and instilled a sense of fear about this subject, instead of making them fall in love with the same. They continue to despise mathematics for the rest of their lives.

A Non-judgemental Approach

Deepa adds how wrong it is to become judgemental about kids and add tags to them, something that sticks with them for life at times. She shares the example of a child who was in the 7th grade and every teacher came and told her that the child could not read and was a poor reader. She talked to the child.

I found out that he had some difficulties with spellings of certain words. I worked with him and communicated with him regularly. Shortly after, he read a chapter in the class and was applauded. The boy is doing very well. No separate exam paper has to be prepared for him like previously when he was branded as a slow learner. If I had approached this kid with all those pre-conceived notions, then he would still be living with that ignominious tag.

According to Deepa, the two kind of students who need maximum help are those who are termed as below average and the one tagged as above average. The former one gets ignored, left out and is humiliated. The child just needs a bit more facilitation and guidance. The latter is among the more curious lot and generally has a lot of questions. You need patience and a bit of empathy to deal effectively.

Half Glass Full

Despite her high credential as a teacher, Deepa has made her own share of mistakes and she is gracious enough to share the same.

There was this child who had been absent for two days and his work was pending. When he turned up after two days and I was collecting notebooks for correction, he stood up and told me that he did not have the homework notebook, so he had done the work in the rough notebook. I was angry with him for having done so. But right at that moment I realized that I had made a mistake. I excused myself for a few minutes from the class and reflected on my response. I realized that the student had told me very happily that he had completed his work in a rough notebook despite not having his homework notebook with him. He could have left the work incomplete, but he chose to do the work in the rough notebook. Instead of appreciating him for this sense of responsibility, I scolded him. I immediately went back to the class and apologized to him. We often focus on what has not been done, instead of looking at what has been done.

Deepa could not have said this more aptly.

Patience, Patience, Patience

Patience is a virtue that teachers need in abundance. Manaswati says,

You need patience to deal with them. I remember sometime back when I scolded a boy in my class, he became very quiet appearing to be hurt. After the lesson was over, I went up to his seat and sat next to him. As soon as I put hand on his shoulders and started to talk to him trying to help him understand his mistake, he started to tremble with anger. I tried to calm him for quite some time, all the while trying to make him realize his mistakes. However, reason was lost on him. I could make out that he was understanding what I was telling him, but he somehow could not reconcile with the fact that I had scolded him. He needed a bit of time. So, after some talking to him for some time, I just walked away and became busy with other class chores. This strategy worked. About 20 minutes later, the same boy walked up to me and apologized. Ever since he has always been respectful towards me and his behaviour has shown marked improvement.

Do Not Hurt Their Self-Esteem

Even in situations of high provocation, there is nothing that prevents a positive disciplining approach that does not hurt their self-esteem. This generation is much more image-conscious, and if their self-esteem is hurt they might disconnect. Manaswati provides a good example of how this could be done when she was dealing with a theft issue in her class.

Some kid was stealing my chocolates. Kids who have birthdays generally bring chocolates for their classmates and teachers. The chocolate for the teacher is generally bigger than those of the classmates. I used to keep the chocolate on my table. For the last couple of times, I was finding it missing after some time. Obviously, some kid in the class was taking it. It is not what you steal that becomes so important, but the behaviour needs correction. I could straight away confront the offender and scold him in front of the class. The next time it happened, I went to the class and instead of asking who had committed the mistake, I told them that I could find out who had taken the chocolate by watching the CCTV footage. But then if I did so, then the vice-principal would also be involved. Instead of that, I just told them to come up to me and tell me later. They could even write and give it to me. After some time, a boy in my class came up to me and after conversing for some time, he quietly pushed a paper chit in my hand. He had written sorry on the chit. I had a quiet chat with him later and the problem was solved.

Being a Mentor

Teachers need to step up their role from just being teachers to being mentors for the zeners. The vulnerability, insecurity and pressures that they go through need a mentor in a teacher to make a positive difference in their lives. Daisy Bastian narrates one such incident:

One of my students, a 10th grade girl, was consistently scoring 30–40 per cent marks and her parents feared that she would fail her board exams. When I talked to the child, I realized that she was highly stressed with a tight evening schedule for swimming and dance classes besides her subject tuitions. Although she enjoyed all these classes, she was physically exhausted, and she had no time left for reading or practising her lessons. After several rounds of conversations, the parents and the child came to an understanding about prioritizing the goals for the year. She adjusted her swimming and dance classes, taking them on alternate days, twice a week, and planned adequate rest, consuming small portions of wholesome snacks at regular intervals and drinking plenty of water. We also discussed the learning techniques. We reviewed the same every week and improvised on the same. The results were amazing—she scored over 82 per cent and remained stress-free and happy.

The New Learning Context

We have been focusing on how the role of a teacher is undergoing a transformation because of the infusion of these new generation of learners in the classroom. However, we should not forget that this new generation of learners and their learning preferences have been shaped by the context and the environment. The environment or the changing world order also makes knowledge dissemination-based teaching and fact-based examinations obsolete. The rote learning method and examining students on the basis of their ability to memorize things and reproduce them on answer sheets serve little purpose in preparing zeners for the world they live in and the world that they will live in, which are vastly different from our previous worlds—volatile, uncertain, complex, ambiguous, hi-tech and where rapid change is the only constant. As I emphasized before, schools are useful only if they can help shape learning and assure that this learning will help these kids in their future life, in solving real-life problems and issues. Else, the whole gamut of schools and education will be a zero-sum game.

The examination system in India and most parts of Asia is so toxic that anything less than 90 per cent in exams is unacceptable. If any student gets less than the magic figure, it almost is labelled as a crime.

'How could you?' 'What will happen to you know?' 'How will you withstand the competition?' are the common ways to stigmatize the achievements of a child. In such times, a mother from Delhi, Vandana Sufia Katoch, won the heart of netizens with her unapologetic post on FB celebrating her son's marks. The post read as follows:

Super proud of my boy who scored a 60% in Class 10 board exams. Yes, it is not a 90, but that doesn't change how I feel. Simply because I have seen him struggle with certain subjects almost to the point of giving up, and then deciding to give his all in the last month-and-a-half to finally make it through! Here's to you, Aamer. And others like you—fishes asked to climb trees. Chart your own course in the big, wide ocean, my love. And keep your innate goodness, curiosity and wisdom alive. And of course, your wicked sense of humour!

While and before writing this book, I had a chance to speak to many zeners. Most of them feel that what they study in schools has low practical relevance in their day-to-day life and do not think that what they are learning will be of much use in the future.

We all pride our respective school education systems. There are strengths of every education system, and we have every reason to feel good about it, as much as others have. But for once, keeping this pride aside, if we think objectively, two things are clear: one, zeners are a different breed of learners (as we saw earlier in the chapter) and second, they will be much better served if they are taught in a manner that allows free thinking and application. The onus is on the teachers to make a difference. There is no denying the fact. But knowing well how much the context plays a role in influencing attitudes and behaviours, in the absence of right context, few good teachers may continue their experimentation with teaching methods and inject innovation in their teaching based on changing needs of learners, but majority will just follow the beaten path. This randomness in application will be defeating one. The only way to ensure that most teachers are motivated and guided to use innovative teaching methods to cater to the learning needs of the zeners, the situation or the context needs to be altered as well.

The Finnish model of school education has always been regarded as revolutionary. They have fewer working hours, give no homework, yet produce great results consistently, which is amazing. For nearly two decades, Finland has enjoyed a reputation of having one of the world's best education systems. Its 15-year-olds regularly score among the highest in the global Programme for International Student Assessment (PISA) league tables for reading, maths and science. However, the latest transformation that Finland has brought about in school education called the 'phenomenon-based learning' is being considered revolutionary. Daisy Bastian says,

I have heard of the phenomena-based learning of Finland and studied about brain-based learning techniques and multidisciplinary learning modules intended to develop competencies. The Finland phenomena is something which has always amazed me. Classes starting late, students playing through the day, with no homework, still achieving great results!

What makes the phenomenon-based learning unique is the 360° shift in the concept and practice of teaching and learning. Till now we have heard about predefined subjects in schools such as science, maths, languages and social sciences. The students are taught concepts based on these subjects and in some cases they may be taught application of these subjects in real-life phenomena. The phenomenon-based learning takes the exact opposite route. Real-world phenomena should be the starting point (pupils ask questions or pose problems)—local, national, global aspects. The duration, extent and methods can vary; there is a holistic approach—all subjects to be integrated. Concepts are taught to explain these phenomena better and integrated learning helps students draw relationship between real-life phenomenon and concepts and between concepts themselves. The learning experiences are contextual, meaningful and real. There should be differentiated, individual learning paths—different learning experiences such as art, language and sports (multiple intelligence). The teaching needs to be centred around the student. The phenomenon-based learning encourages collaborative peer learning.

From August 2016 it has become compulsory for every Finnish school to use collaborative teaching methods, allowing students to choose a topic (phenomenon) relevant to them and base subjects around it. They then make innovative use of technology and sources outside the school to gather information about the phenomenon they have selected. The outside sources can include experts, museums or research. The purpose is to prepare students for changes in the surrounding world, to help them learn skills and information which are directly applicable to life and to motivate students to understand the purpose of learning. Also known as project-based learning, the students have chosen some of the biggest issues confronting Europe as phenomena or projects, such as immigration, Brexit and climate change, to name a few.

•What's unusual about Finnish schools?	•Teaching is a highly respected, well-paid profession
	•There are no school inspections or teacher evaluations
	•The school system is highly centralised and most schools are publicly funded.
	•School days are short and the summer break is 10 weeks
	•Children are assessed by their teachers. The only nationwide exam is for those who continue studying to 18
	•Average school size is 195 pupils; average class size is 19 pupils

Source: BBC.com, retrieved from https://www.bbc.com/news/world-europe-39889523 (accessed on 22 Nov 2019).

Sceptics will always be there and will wonder how this drastic change impacts the results and performance of the students. But I think this is the disruption we needed in the school educational landscape, especially with zeners populating them. For those who are sceptical, let me ask you one question? How much of what you studied in school do you remember using in your daily life? The lack of a good answer to this question should be the first reason to put scepticism to rest.

Whether we are ready for phenomenon-based learning or we are moving towards it by ensuring at least practice-based learning, we need to alter the learning context, which will in turn have a full-scale impact on the teaching process, methods and approaches. Remember that the clock is ticking and we are losing the opportunity to make a difference in the lives of zeners when it comes to their school education and preparing them for their life, career and world. Learn, innovate, adopt and change.

4
THE DIGITAL DILEMMA

A rnab was playing a game on my laptop. It seemed like a quiz game but concerned why he was using my laptop for playing games, I interrupted him. To my surprise and amazement, I found him playing a quiz game that he had developed himself. Arnab, who has just stepped into his teens, used a simple programming language Basic-256 to develop the game. He had also developed two other games, one of them being a word power game. Arnab, who had been taught the basic of Basic-256 this year at his school, explored the language on his own and used it to develop games. The games, although very basic, were interesting. In fact, he made me play those games as well. When his computer teacher came to know about his exploits, she was very proud of him and commended him for the application. Baby steps for Arnab but there is nothing doubting the fact that digital and mobile technologies open a vast realm of opportunities for the generation of kids who have been born in its cradle.

Self-Learning

Take the case of Nihar Thakkar, a fourteen-year-old boy from Bengaluru, a school dropout and a homeschooler who has developed an app to track the city buses in real time. The app called 'Bengaluru Buses—Track BMTC Buses in real-time' has become a hit among the commuters, eclipsing the official BMTC (Bangalore Metropolitan Transport Corporation) app that people call redundant and inaccurate. Nihar's app has already seen more than 60,000 downloads, with an average of 8,000 new downloads every month. Strong positive reviews of the app from the users are a testimonial of his efforts. He used real-time data of the buses from the BMTC server and also gathered information about pre-fixed timings of buses to develop the app. Nihar, all but fourteen years of age, did what BMTC could not and the school could not teach him, on his own—thanks to the transformational technologies that exist these days.

The amount of information and knowledge that is available at the tap of a finger is unimaginable. Most kids of this generation have tremendous knowledge in areas of their interest. I have often been dumbfounded at the amount of knowledge these kids have about certain things, which they have gathered on their own using mobile and the Internet. I genuinely feel that gone are the days when kids needed to go to school to gain knowledge. Enough and more knowledge is available online. Schools are more seats of learning or maybe they should change from knowledge disseminators to learning hubs.

Such knowledge available online today has made self-learning among children possible from an early age, although at times these abilities can boomerang too. An Australian teenager who dreamt of working for the tech-giant Apple recently pleaded guilty to hacking into the firm's main computer network, downloading big internal files and accessing customer accounts. When Apple became aware of the intrusion, the case was referred to US FBI, who in turn referred the matter to the Australian Federal Police (AFP). The AFP raid at the boy's house recovered two laptops, a mobile phone and a hard drive that he used for hacking. However, the boy had not leaked any of the information. The issue is sub judice. What will you call this—Apple's inability that its network could be hacked by a teenage boy or the super ability of an unguided/misguided teenager?

When guided properly by adults especially parents, such technologies can help kids learn in a significant way, mostly in a self-learning mode. Take the case of virtual piggy banks. A British start-up has designed digital pocket money app. The app called gohenry is a part of the growing range of digital money apps combined with prepaid cards for kids as young as six years old. They have powerful money management and saving tools that replace the old-fashioned piggy banks and passbooks. When kids have money, they want to spend it quickly, but the app lets them check their balances online which actually makes them start thinking about saving rather than getting rid of all their money. Parents also prefer to give digital allowances rather than physical cash. Alipay and WeChat in China, Octopus Card in Hong Kong, Nimbl and Osper in UK, Spriggy and Family Zoo in Australia, and Greenlight in the USA are part of this growing virtual piggy-bank tribe.

Fun @Learning

Mobile and digital technologies have made gamification a reality and have the potential to transform traditional learning that is often boring into fun and exciting. Games are exceptional tools for supplementing the way information is taught in school. Through imaginative contexts and the use of game mechanics, concepts become alive and engaging. More so because such apps enable self-learning and are not dependent on school curriculums or teacher's assistance, although now there are increasing suggestions how the concept and practice of gamification should be applied in school education as well.

Esports are becoming common in the USA and universities are increasingly treating esports equal to other sports. Multiplayer video games played competitively often with spectators are known as esports, and they have increasingly become a gateway to college scholarship money. Teenage students play these games competitively and the winner wins the scholarship. Over the past few years, the National Association of Collegiate Esports, which is connected with 98 university programmes across the USA and Canada, has facilitated $16 million in scholarships. Games competitively viable in the collegiate sphere have real depth and deep levels of strategy, and require strategic teamwork and real mastery to be successful. Using gaming for awarding scholarships matches with this generation's preference and proficiency for playing such games, and the fact that it tests real skills makes the whole process of earning scholarships fun.

Even if learning is fun for children, exams are seldom fun for them. Stress is naturally associated with exams. But now there is a mobile app to help these children overcome exam stress, anxiety and depression. Conquer Exams is a mobile application created by the Indian Institute of Public Health working in collaboration with the National Mental Health Programme, Department of Family Welfare and Government of Gujarat in India. Exams and exam results severely stress the students, and considering how susceptible zeners are to such stress often leading to depression and at times even suicides, this mobile app is an attempt to reach out to the students on the platforms that they frequent and make exams fun as well. The students are encouraged to answer a questionnaire through a tab called 'dot your apprehension' to assess the stress levels. Based on the risk level, the app advises them to seek counselling or dial Jeevan Aastha, a professional counselling toll free number. There is a module for parents as well. The idea is to provide mental health immunity and improve coping levels of students and parents.

Learning at the Tip of the Finger

Mobile and digital technologies have made learning possible at the tap of the finger. Mobile-based applications such as BYJU's and NEETprep have changed the entire landscape of coaching, offering such solutions to students at the comfort of their home, allowing them to log in at times they are comfortable. Live online classes, gamification of learning, use of videos and augmented reality interactive learning methods, and all of that at literally your fingertips is transforming the coaching institution. NEETprep claims that over 10 million video lecture minutes are consumed by over 0.25 million students every month.

MOOCs are yet another revolution in learning facilitated by mobile and digital technologies. Gone are the days when only a select few had access to the best universities and academic institutions around the world. MOOC platforms such as Udemy, Coursera, Udacity and Alison have provided a gateway for zeners and millennials alike to the altars of the top universities via the online digital platform. Courses in AI, machine learning, analytics and a whole range of interest areas are available for enrolment, many of them even free of cost.

Inclusive Learning

Despite the advancements in technology, modern forms of learning have yet to become inclusive when it comes to integrating the vast mass of rural students who do not have privileges as the urban students. Mobile and digital technology is helping bridge this gap. The efforts of Shivakumar M., a national award-winning teacher in a government high school in rural Karnataka, has helped rural students learn mathematics in a fun, interactive manner. Shivakumar has developed three maths learning applications in the local language, Kannada—SSLC passing package, Interactive Quiz and Basic Mathematics—which has helped many students. Most other maths learning apps were available in English and weren't accessible to the rural students. But Shivakumar ensured that these apps were available in the local language through a YouTube channel. Interestingly, Shivakumar comes from a non-technical background, and using the technology-assisted learning programme (TALP) training that he underwent and the NCERT maths books, he created the apps that are also being used by his other colleagues teaching in other village government schools.

Had it not been for such technologies, a bright student like Nishka would have never made beyond the horizon of her abilities. Nishka's speech was impaired and right-hand movement was restricted since she was eight years old when she was infected by a rare hereditary condition that manifested as dystonia. After losing two academic years, she enrolled in a special school. Her condition did not allow her to transcribe her own answers in an examination nor could she dictate the answer to an additional transcriber. With support from her academic institution and board of studies, she was allowed to type the answer on an iPad using a single finger of her left hand and the writer then transcribed it on the answer sheet.

Skills for the Future

Mobile and digital technologies and their easy accessibility are helping the current generation of kids and adolescents to acquire skills for the future. In another 10 years, many jobs that exist today may not be there and new jobs will emerge that would require a whole different array of skills. In an era of automation, digitization and AI, the skill directory is undergoing a transformation, starting from coding to machine learning, SEO/SEM, mobile development, cyber-security specialists and many more. No wonder the Indian government is planning digitization of classrooms at school as well as college level under the project 'Operation Digital Board' (ODB).

New Talent Platform

Mobile and digital apps are also helping many kids to showcase their talent to the world without necessarily being dependent on the traditional media, which is often crowded and is also losing its mass appeal. We are living in an era of web series and entertainment apps such as Netflix and Amazon Prime, not to forget our very own friendly neighbourhood YouTube. These digital mediums make it possible for users to showcase their talent to the world using minimum technology infrastructure. There are many kids who are celebrities now, thanks to their YouTube videos. Most zeners have their own YouTube channels and followers on Instagram. My son gets better followers on Instagram than myself, not to mention his YouTube channel 'Skeleton Music', where he initially used to post the cover versions of popular songs of his favourite Alan Walker, and he is now preparing to launch his own original single online.

Mobile and digital technologies have helped Gen Z to stay connected, and obviously it is their biggest source of entertainment as well. TV is losing favour among zeners, and user-driven content viewing is ruling the roost.

Grass Is Not So Green on the Other Side

However, the picture is not all that rosy. The benefits of technology are not hidden from anyone; however, the banes of technology are not known to all. The overuse of mobile and gadgets comes with adverse effects. Technology addiction is common among people these days, especially among the younger generation. Such addiction has social, emotional, psychological and physical implications on the individual and on the society as a whole. The kids and adolescents are the worst affected. How do we identify an addiction to technology gadgets or social media, why we should be concerned about such addiction and what can we do to address such addiction?

Nomophobia

The other day, browsing through social media, I came across a video that depicted a new product. A mobile with a spoon and fork (spelt as Spoon_phork in the video). The spoon and fork fold at the back of the mobile and are also detachable. When someone wants to eat and do phone at the same time, he/she will no longer have to keep alternating between phone and fork or phone and spoon. He/she can use the phone and at the same time use the fork that folds out from the lower end of the phone and eat with it too. Marketed as a product that will reduce disposable usage on earth, this is the worst product innovation that I have come across in recent times. In an era when mobile addiction is becoming a global epidemic, this product would further encourage people to be stuck to their phones even while eating.

Do you know this word called nomophobia? Even if you do not, chances are that you either have experienced this condition yourself or know someone suffering from it. A term that was coined during a 2010 study by the UK Post Office, nomophobia means the fear of being without a mobile device. The 'no mobile phone phobia' is growing among adults, kids and adolescents alike. The thought of being without a mobile phone in this world sets off a panic button for most people. What if my phone runs out of charge? What if I forget my mobile at home? What if my mobile data does not work? What if the place I am going to visit or the hotel that I am going to stay in does not have Wi-Fi? How will I use my phone then? This constant fear of being 'stranded' without a mobile phone is nomophobia. During a study, the UK Post Office found the majority of respondents suffering from anxieties of losing their mobile phones or running out of battery or having no network coverage/Wi-Fi.

Food for TV

Bonshila Dhar, an IT specialist-cum-homemaker, has totally banned mobile phone for her four-year-old son Nihaan and has restricted TV watching to maximum of 30 minutes a day, amid fears that her son was using these gadgets too much. Bonshila is well aware of the hazards that such overuse poses to kids. She narrates the ways in which Nihaan tries to extend and maximize his TV-viewing time. Nihaan, who is only allowed to watch TV when he is having his food, takes longer to finish his food so that he could have few extra minutes of TV. One evening, when Nihaan was watching his favourite cartoons on TV, his father Surojit came back from office. Surojit told Nihaan that as he had been watching cartoon for quite some time, he wanted to instead catch up with some news. As soon as Surojit switched the channel, Nihaan went running to his mom and asked for his dinner to be served. Bonshila was surprised as it was not his dinner time yet, but Nihaan was adamant. When Bonshila agreed to serve him dinner, he immediately asked for his cartoon channel to be restored on TV as he would then have his food. This privilege was refused by his parents as he had already finished his quota of watching TV that day. By the time Bonshila returned from kitchen with Nihaan's dinner plate, she found that her boy had dozed-off on the sofa. The only motivation for Nihaan seemed to be TV, and being denied the same, he had lost interest in having dinner.

Nihaan is all but four years old, and his aware parents will in all possibility groom him in a way that he learns to use these technologies and gadgets more responsibly and in a manner that does not hurt his prospects. But is this true for most other kids? Fears of mobile and gadget addiction rule supreme, and fears of the consequent adverse impact on their health and future are not misplaced.

Addicted?

Children and adults getting addicted to mobile, gadgets and technology is very common these days. But how to know whether one is addicted or not? The international classification of mobile or smartphone addiction/digital addiction states three parameters to define addiction.

1. **Loss of Control:** When a person loses his/her control over choosing time, duration and place of mobile usage, this is termed as loss of control.
2. **Predominant Activity:** Mobile/digital activity becomes the predominant activity in a person's life. Other activities, even the more important ones, take a backseat.
3. **Use, Despite Harm:** Despite knowing that using a mobile for a long duration may cause harm to self, one continues to use/abuse the gadget.

When these symptoms persist in a person for 12 months or more, then it can be safely stated that he/she is addicted to mobile/gadget. This can also be termed as digital addiction.

The 5C Addiction Test

'Teen hangs himself after father refuses to buy cellphone', screamed the morning headline of a popular English daily. No, this is not fiction or an attempt to sensationalize the text. This is an unfortunate reality that is hitting us hard. In this case, the sixteen-year-old boy could not take a 'no' from his father, who asked him to wait till he finished his 10th grade exams. Adamant to have a cell phone, he took the refusal badly and killed himself.

This is an extreme case of mobile addiction, where the compulsion and craving are so high that they end in a tragedy. To avert such tragedies and to ensure that our kids and adolescents do not reach the point of addiction to mobile and digital technology, we must first understand what defines addiction.

Dr Manoj Kumar Sharma, Consultant Psychologist at NIMHANS, has developed another metric for defining mobile/gadget/digital/technology addiction, which is more descriptive than the international classification. Dr Sharma calls it the 5C model.

1. **Craving:** A constant, strong and irrepressible craving for mobile.

2. **Control (loss of control):** Not being able to self-regulate time, duration and place of mobile usage.
3. **Coping mechanism:** Using mobile as a coping mechanism— mobile for relaxation, mobile for warding off boredom, mobile for dealing with sadness, etc.
4. **Compulsion:** Mobile becomes a compulsive habit. One feels a sense of compulsion to use it as if his/her life depends on it.
5. **Consequences:** Despite knowing the harmful consequences of overuse/abuse of mobile phones and digital technology, one continues to use it over long hours.

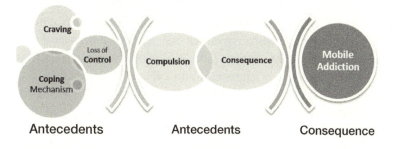

Dr Sharma states that if at least 4 out of 5 Cs persist for 6–12 months, then it means the person is addicted.

Gaming is another major addiction linked to mobile/gadget/technology addiction among children. Dr Sharma says that gaming is a vicious cycle. What begins more as an entertainment ends up in addiction, with some children getting used to the screen for 10–12 hours a day. This severely affects their sleep cycle, food intake, academics and interpersonal communication. At SHUT Clinic in NIMHANS, Dr Sharma gets on an average six children every week addicted to gaming from various states of India, seeking help.

PUBG or PlayerUnknown's Battlegrounds is an online multi-player game where about 100 players fight in a free-for-all combat, where the sole survivor emerges victorious. PUBG has become a rage around the world with more than 100 million downloads of the game. And its addiction among kids and teenagers has become one of the most debatable topics. There have been calls to ban the game as it is said to be severely addictive.

Few months back, an eighteen-year-old boy in Mumbai committed suicide when he was denied a high-end smartphone that he was demanding to play a PUBG game. The teenager wanted a phone costing nearly ₹37,000 to play the addictive online game. His family however did not heed his request and refused to give him a phone costing more than ₹20,000. Feeling distraught, the teenager took this extreme step.

Gujarat, a state in the western part of India, issued a notice to ban PUBG in primary schools, while in another western state of the country, Maharashtra, an eleven-year-old boy submitted a plea in the high court through his mother to seek a ban on the game as it promotes violence, aggression and cyberbullying. Gujarat was the first state to order a blanket ban on the PUBG game over concerns about its impact on the behaviour, conduct and language of people playing the game. Post enforcement of the ban, few students who were found playing the game were arrested by the police and later released on bail. The funny thing is that the police reported that the students were so 'engrossed' in playing the game that they did not even notice the cops coming. In another such incident, two youths were run over by a train as they sat on the railway track so absorbed in playing the game that they did not see or hear the train coming.

Facing the heat from all ends, the Chinese gaming giant Tencent—maker of the PUBG game—imposed a digital lock on some of its games that require players under 13 years of age to ask their guardians to open the game. But we all know to what extent such features will work. This generation is far smarter to be stopped by such flimsy security features. They know passwords of their parents and not vice versa. And in many cases parents are themselves addicted to their phones and even gaming.

In a recent incident reported from the central part of India from a state called Madhya Pradesh, a young boy was so busy playing PUBG that he picked up a bottle of acid instead of water and drank it, and suffered major internal burns. An emergency surgery performed on his intestines could save his life.

Dr Sharma adds,

Addicted kids take the virtual world to be real and cannot tolerate anyone questioning them. There are multiplayer online games where users don't know one another and are from different countries. They feel associated to this virtual family but ignore their immediate family in the process.

The seriousness of the problem cannot be emphasized any more than the fact that the World Health Organization (WHO) has declared gaming addiction a mental disorder.

The Triggers of Mobile Addiction

Although born in the cradle of technology, zeners do not get addicted to the same on their own. Like every behaviour, addiction too has its causes.

It will not be incorrect to say that parents are the number one cause of mobile addiction among kids. Most of this addiction happens by the age of five and continues thereafter. Hence, for most of the zeners addicted to mobile and technology, the addiction starts at home. Parents influence this addiction in many ways. The advent of smartphone has made phone more than a calling device; in fact, the mobile is everything but a calling device. Parents use this mobile as a toy to engage the child and make him/her follow instructions.

Mobile Feeds

Ayesha, a two-year-old child of Anisha and Adil, is a bit fussy about her food, as most kids of her age are. Feeding her is not the easiest task. She throws tantrums whenever her parents try to feed her. Like every worried parent, Anisha and Adil have been trying to find a solution to this problem, so that their growing baby gets the right nutrition. It is said that necessity is the mother of all inventions. Adil has found an 'innovative' way to keep Ayesha engaged and feed her. Now whenever he feeds Ayesha, both his hands are engaged. While one hand is busy feeding her with spoon, the other hand holds the mobile where he plays her favourite cartoon video from YouTube. Mobile has a spellbound effect on Ayesha, and she simply keeps staring at the screen. Meanwhile, Adil completes feeding her. It is so 'easy' now! The other day Anisha tried feeding her but she did not have the mobile with her as it was put on charge. Ayesha simply refused to eat. Earlier, with some cajoling, storytelling or by loving persuasion, Ayesha would eat. But now those techniques do not work. Anisha had to wait till her mobile was charged enough to play a video and only then did Ayesha finish her meal.

Heard about classical conditioning? Ayesha's case is not an isolated one. Mobile has become an easy way out. When these kids grow up and are glued to mobile screens, we blame them. How ironical!

Drugged

Sumeet and Sunaina, a couple with a five-year-old child Ruby, had just joined their friends Gagan-Gunjan, Mayank-Meena, Pakanj-Palak, Keertan-Kavya and Rohit-Rubina for a get-together. All of them had kids like Sumeet and Sunaina. It was New Year's Eve. The get-together was at Gagan-Gunjan's house. The evening had just started. There were lots of plans for the evening—drinks, game of cards, few couple games, couple dances. Meanwhile, the kids had all holed-up in another room. They were noisy as usual. Screaming, singing, dancing, playing, all at the same time. Occasionally, a fight broke out between a few of them. Then one of them started crying, came running to complain what the other kid had done to them. Parents had to respond to the 'emergency' and douse the 'fire' to restore normalcy again. The drinks and conversations were getting interrupted, time and again, because of this clamour. Ruby came running next from the kid's room. 'Papa, Papa, Papa ... Nitin is beating me,' sobbing she narrated her plight to her father Sumeet. After consoling Ruby, Sumeet gave his phone to Ruby, and she started playing a game sitting in a corner. Gradually, this practice was emulated by other parents too. Suddenly, the entire house fell silent. All kids had now phones of their dad or mum. Each of them had found a corner for himself or herself. They were engrossed in the phone. This became a routine whenever get-togethers would occur. The kids would be given phones, and they would be quiet through the evening, even eat without fuss, leaving adults with time and space to do their 'stuff'. No disturbance, no noise, no firefighting, it was all so peaceful.

A mobile phone is often used as a bribe. Phones work in the same way a drug does; they have the same sedative effect. Once a child gets a phone, peculiarly they fall silent, huddle in a corner and remain glued to it for hours together. And hence phones have become a convenient way for parents to bribe their kids to remain silent and not disturb them while they are busy. Finnish scientist Lea Hyvarinen says that gadgets, including smartphones, are like a pacifier for a child, but the negatives are progressive myopia cases and rise in attention-deficit hyperactivity disorders among children.

Dr Sharma says that it is indeed a matter of concern how parents hand over the phone to the child. Such a complicated device is handed over to the kids, which plays with their emotions, stimulates their hormones and creates a virtual world for them. Yet parents forget to educate the kids about do's and don'ts. There is hardly any regulation or guidance on how to use phone, what to do and what practices are not desirable.

Sometimes, I wonder whether most parents themselves understand the do's and don'ts of using mobile technology. I often find young adults addicted to their phones. Children use their parents as their first role model. No wonder they start following their parent's footsteps even when it comes to mobile usage.

Shortkut

'Do you want to order from KFC?' the WhatsApp message from Dad interrupted the game that Arihant was playing with his online friends. A bit irritated yet not being able to resist the KFC temptation, Arihant texted back, 'K'.

Rishabh saw the text and was angry—What was happening to the language and etiquettes of this generation? They can't even type Ok. Thank You. Just K? What is this?

Anyways, Rishabh, who was on his way back from office, ordered online the evening snacks from KFC. Once back home, he decided to give a pep talk to his son Arihant. Here's how the conversation went.

Rishabh: Arihant, is this how you respond to people? What is this K?

Arihant: K means Ok.

Rishabh: Don't you even have time to write 'Ok. Thank You.'

Arihant: But Dad, you understood, right? Then what's the problem?

Rishabh: It is not the question of understanding. Manners, Arihant?

Arihant: But even mom writes Thank You as 'Thnq'. What's wrong?

Rishabh: Wrong is your attitude. You should be more polite.

Arihant: I was playing a game when you texted. You interrupted me.

Rishabh: You are arguing instead of understanding my point.

Arihant: C'mon Dad, I was playing a game.

Rishabh: You are losing etiquettes and right language, both together.

Arihant: And the other day you wrote 'LOL'.

Before Arihant could complete, Rishabh shouted at him and asked him to shut up. Arihant kept quiet after that, not convinced though and very angry with his Dad. He decided to use that kind of lingo more often then on.

While Rishabh's concern is valid, he should not forget that kids model their parents. Even the way parents use mobile, their texting lingo and their discipline with the gadget are all copied consciously or subconsciously by the kids.

Mobile becomes a priority in most houses. There is some sense of FOMO or fear of missing out. And there is a compulsive drive to attend even unimportant calls or check WhatsApp notifications and FB likes every few minutes. When parents put mobile over the child in terms of priority, the child also learns the same.

'Smart' Phoney

Dorothy is a four-year-old girl. She has just started going to school. Every day when she comes back from school, she is all so excited to tell her mother about her day. Dorothy's conversations with her mother are often interrupted by phone calls or social media pop-up notifications. Her mom then rushes  to take the call or answer to the message. By the time the call ends, both Dorothy and her mom forget about the conversation that is often left incomplete. At times, Dorothy feels that her mother's phone was her enemy, which always plotted to take her mother's attention away from her. Once she even tried to hide the phone but then it screamed loudly when the call came, even from under the pillow where she had hidden it, and her mother once again went away to attend the call. 'The phone was really smart', thought Dorothy, 'a wee bit smart'.

What do you think Dorothy will do when she grows up? It will be no surprise if Dorothy does the same with her parents. She will remain busy with her mobile attending to it first, while her mother will go hoarse calling her for breakfast or for doing her daily chores. After all, it was she who implicitly communicated to her that 'mobile was more important'.

There are many single-child families where both parents are working. The child spends plenty of time alone in the house, especially after coming back from school, till at least one of the parents comes back home. Boredom and loneliness are common in such kids. Worse, when parents come back home they themselves spend a lot of time on phone. Mobile is often used as a reward these days for kids or as a coping mechanism. The child learns to cope with loneliness or boredom with mobile. It becomes a way to feel happy; all recreation is through mobile; even the child learns to share his/her feelings or stories with the mobile (virtual world). In short, mobile becomes the child's best friend. A gadget with no emotions, and one that can open windows to an unknown virtual world, becoming the best friend of a child is extremely concerning.

Birthday Gift

Prince had turn ten and was excited about his birthday present. His father had bought him a smartphone. How exciting! He thought, 'I will be able to do Instagram, WhatsApp, play games and now I do not have to request my mom or dad to borrow their phone to do all that. I can do as much as I like.' Prince was right in his prediction. He had all the time with his phone that he could possibly imagine. The only time he could not use his phone was during his school hours and sleep time. Slowly, Prince stopped going outdoors for play during evenings. His football friends got tired of waiting for him and calling out his name from downstairs every day. Prince had a new set of friends. They were his online virtual friends. He used to play online games with them, chat with them, and make

videos and post them on his YouTube channel. Evenings had changed in his house. His dad and mom, both of whom worked, used to come late from office. He no more felt bored. He used to talk to his phone, play with it and watch videos. His phone had become his best friend. Weekends had changed too. Earlier, everyone—Prince and his dad and mom—would watch TV together, occasionally play board games or just chit-chat about the whole week. Later, everyone was busy on their respective phones. Even on dinner table they did not talk much. After all, notifications kept popping up on phone, every now and then. Within a year, Prince had changed. His body weight had increased. He had become slower and lazier. His entire body language had changed. Oh, did I tell you, Prince has a new accessory now—his reading glasses?

Adolescent zeners or slightly older kids often start using mobile, giving in to peer pressure. Because other kids use mobile, the one who does not becomes the odd one out. Often they become targets of social ridicule. How kids react to such pressures depends a lot on the atmosphere at home. If their self-esteem is not boosted by the parents or if the parents themselves are guilty of being addicted to their phones, then kids have a greater chance of falling prey to such peer pressures.

Mobile also ensures private accessibility for the zeners. They can browse content in private. Often older kids and adolescents are exposed to sensitive and inappropriate material online. Addiction to pornography at a young age is becoming common because of lack of guidance, curiosity to know the 'unknown' and an opportunity to do all that in private. Once they are addicted to such material, they find themselves trapped. Even if they want to wriggle out of the addiction, it is difficult. They find it difficult to talk about the same with their parents or other elders. They themselves cannot overcome this addiction. In such a scenario, they only slump deeper into the crisis. Recently, a village in a conservative region of Indonesia decided to pull the plug on wireless Internet after they found the village children accessing porn sites instead of going through holy book verses. While pulling the plug over Wi-Fi is definitely not the solution, it just goes on to show how much harm unguided, unrestricted access to digital mediums can cause.

The 'lonely child' phenomenon is very common these days. Not to say that it happens in every household, but it is true that many households create 'lonely child' either because both the parents are working and too busy with their work or because they are too busy with their phones or gadgets themselves, leaving very less time to spend with their kids. Dr Sharma tells that these days children even under the age of five years feel lonely in some cases. Mobile addiction in such kids starts with mobile becoming a coping gadget. Poor academic performance, poor relationships, loneliness, boredom, all find solace with phone. The child somehow infers, 'The world is not fair to me. No one listens to me, no one understand me. Only my phone listens to whatever I have to say.' Such deductions are presumably dangerous.

Impact on Physical Well-Being

Doctors point out to the kind of serious damage that excessive mobile usage can do the zeners. Among the first to get affected is the vision.

Senior eye specialist Dr Savitha Arun, consultant anterior segment and electro physiology dealing with paediatric ophthal-mology, medical superintendent and member of the board of directors at Nethradhama hospital, Bengaluru, provides startling insights into how excessive mobile usage and screen time are ravaging the vision of kids and adolescents.

The Computer Vision Syndrome

Computer vision syndrome, unheard in kids and adolescents few years back, can be seen in paediatric patients increasingly. Computer vision syndrome is linked to excessive screen time that causes eye strain, eye ache, a continuous nagging sensation, headache and dryness of eyes. Those who develop computer vision syndrome find it difficult to switch from screen to printed text and hence have an aversion to 'near work'.

Computer vision syndrome was prevalent only in software engi-neers. However, now, our kids and adolescents are also affected. Dr Savitha adds, 'Parents have a habit of showing mobile phones playing games or videos in them while feeding them.' This habit grows as the kids grow. Later they develop a habit of watching TV or playing with mobile phones even while eating or doing other import-ant work. As a result, their concentration is more on the mobile rather than on the food. This makes them poor eaters and impacts their nutrition and health. Parents can provide various reasons why they showed mobile to kids while feeding them or to keep them busy or occupied. But most experts including Dr Savitha say that none of the excuses are acceptable and almost all of them are avoidable.

Blinkers On!

Frequent blinking of eyes by kids and adolescents is another problem arising out of excessive mobile/gadget usage. This not only becomes a social nuisance but is also a sign of bad times ahead for the eyes. Normally, a person blinks 18–20 times per minute. During each blink, the cornea is resurfaced with tears. However, if that does not happen, then dry spots develop on the cornea, leading to a gritty sensation. When there is excessive mobile usage and sharp rise in screen time, it creates dry spots on the cornea. Frequent blinking is a response to the same, aimed at reducing dry spots. What begins with an involuntary response to dryness of eyes eventually becomes a habit. Such kids find themselves to be the butt of jokes and caustic laughter at their weird habit. Medically, such kids become dependent on tear lubricating drops and even at times on other medicines like immunomodulatory drops.

The Bespectacled Generation

However, the most dangerous impact of rampant mobile usage among kids and adolescents is the progression of myopia. Myopia is now a worldwide epidemic. Since 1971, the incidences of short-sightedness have nearly doubled to 42 per cent. In Asia, up to 90 per cent of teenagers and adults are short-sighted.

Dr Savitha informs how she has seen a steep rise in kids coming with progression of myopia problem, something that was unheard of in them six–seven years back. Every six months, kids come to the hospital only to discover that their 'power' grows by leaps and bounds. Parents of such kids complain of excessive screen time and mobile usage. Alarmingly, more and more children are becoming myopic and most of them are experiencing progression of myopia. Dr Savitha adds that the problem of progression of myopia is likely to further worsen in kids by the year 2020. The problem is a global issue, although more acute in Asia.

It took the highest leadership in China to put a check on online games in China. Alarmed by reports that many Chinese children need glasses, leader Xi Jinping directed China's media regulator to limit the number of new games approved for distribution. It also encourages the regulator to look for measures to limit the amount of time minors can spend playing games. The move reportedly has wiped out billions of dollars from the market value of the world's largest video game company—Tencent. Now we all know who is making billions at the cost of our children. But then we cannot blame them alone or the children. As adults and parents, we set an example for them, often which is not the correct one.

Even adults are not immune to such problems. Dr Savitha talks about the growing incidences of adult onset myopia. In other words, earlier the power would stabilize in people by the time they would reach the age of eighteen years. However, now she gets patients who develop myopia after the age of eighteen years.

Kids and adolescents who develop myopia due to excessive mobile usage and also experience progression of myopia become dependent on medicines and find their eyesight deteriorating early in their life. Dr Savitha reports that close to 75 per cent of kids who come to hospital with a vison issue are connected directly or indirectly with excessive mobile usage. That is worrisome. Kids are no different when it comes to digital eye strain. The symptoms include dry eyes, eye strain, headache and blurry vision.

Besides vision problems, obesity and susceptibility to diseases and infection are also disturbing physical well-being. Lack of outdoor activities, easy availability of junk food, not paying attention to the food they are eating, etc., have resulted in poor body image and rising obesity among this generation.

The doctors feel that there has been in general a fall in personal hygiene levels among zeners. High mobile activity, mostly spending time alone, low social connect and less social activity have contributed to falling personal hygiene that begets infections and diseases easily.

Impact on Cognitive Development

Researchers in the USA, Canada and France have found a clear link among excess 'screen time', early exposure to mobile and gadgets and poor cognitive skills among kids. The strong link between time spent staring at the screen and brain function potentially reflects the interruption of the stress recovery cycle needed for growth in children. Each minute of time spent on screen takes away a minute from sleep. Too little sleep and excess screen time are clearly linked to a drop off in cognitive skills, such as language ability, memory and task completion, besides raising concern about rise in attention deficit hyperactivity disorder among kids.

The problem of excess screen time because of overuse of mobile, digital technology and TV is universal. A study by Jeremy Walsh, a researcher at the Children's Hospital of Eastern Ontario Research Institute, found that only 1 in 20 kids in the USA meets guidelines on sleep, exercise and screen time. On an average, children aged eight–eleven years spend 3.6 hours per day glued to a TV, mobile phone, tablet or computer screen, against the recommended 2 hours. That's almost double the recommended limit.

ABCD is a landmark study on brain development and child health supported by the National Institutes of Health (NIH), USA. This project has recruited nearly 10,000 kids to follow them into early adulthood and understand the impact of environmental, social, genetic and other biological factors on brain and cognitive development and that can enhance or disrupt a young person's life trajectory. In brain scans of 4,500 children, daily screen usage of more than seven hours showed premature thinning of the brain cortex, the outermost layer, which processes information from the physical world. The difference is significant from children who spend less time on screen. According to lead researcher Dr Gaya Dowling, it may be too soon to draw linkages between thinning of brain cortex and cognitive development of kids; however, early results from the ABCD study show that children who spent more than two hours of daily screen time scored lower on thinking and language tests.

Paediatricians from France and the USA urge parents not to allow children any screen time until the age of eighteen months. Canada is the first country to propose time limits on backlit screen.

Dr Girish H. C. and Dr Anil M. U., both prominent consultant paediatricians in Bengaluru, feel that the overexposure to mobile/ gadgets and consequently to the digital world has somewhere diminished personal connect and replaced the same by a digital connect. The kids and adolescents of this generation are more connected to the virtual world than to the real world. The influence that this virtual world is having on them is disturbing and even at times dangerous. Too much use of mobile/gadgets from a very young age creates its own sets of problems.

Speech Delay

Speech delay is becoming a big issue among young kids with the advent of the mobile and digital world. It is not uncommon to find a two-year-old getting worried about the presence of Wi-Fi wherever they go, even to a hospital. As young as three-year-olds are unable to express even to their parents. They take in information but are unable to express the same. Speech delays among kids are common these days. From a very young age, they learn to communicate with the virtual world where speech or oral communication has little role. This is what doctors call the digital disconnect. According to a report published by the American Academy of Pediatrics, heavy use of electronic media might interfere with a child's speech and language development, and replace important playtime with parents, leading to obesity. Paediatricians further recommend no screen time for children up to the age of two years. The screen time includes TV, computers, mobile, tablets and other such electronic gadgets. However, if not restricted from the very beginning, screen time can overwhelm children, making it difficult to control later on. Paediatricians recommend puzzles, balls, colouring books, card games and even empty cardboard boxes as ideal toys for young children.

Clouding Memory and Thinking Abilities

For years, people contemplated the impact of mobile phone radiation on children. Now research proves that mobile phone radiations can indeed impact the memory performance in children and adolescents. Mobile phone is a source of radio frequency electro-magnetic fields (RF-EMF). When mobile phones are used close to the head, they expose the brain to RF-EMF radiations more. Researchers have found in their study that cumulative RF-EMF brain exposure from mobile phone usage over a period of one year may have a negative effect on the development of figural memory performance in children and adolescents. Figural memory is pri-marily located in the right brain hemisphere and hence kids who hold the phone on the right side get impacted more. Other mobile functions such as messaging, playing games and browsing the Internet cause limited exposure of the brain to RF-EMF.

The advent of smartphones, tablets and digital gadgets in our lives has meant a more sedentary life. For zeners who were born in the cradle of digital technology, this has meant large-scale ignorance of outdoor activities. Hours of sitting with the phone or with other digital gadgets is common. Beyond making the kids obese, now research proves that sitting for long hours can affect memory too. According to a new study published in the *Journal of Applied Physiology*, sitting for hours without moving can slow the flow of blood to our brains. Short-term drops in blood flow can temporarily cloud thinking and memory, while longer-term declines are linked to higher risks of neurodegenerative diseases, including dementia. Brain cells need oxygen and nutrients that blood contains, and frequent two-minute walking breaks in between can go a long way in keeping blood flow to the brain intact. However, most kids glued to their phones keep sitting at one place, many times even forgetting to change their posture or to eat. This can have serious consequences.

Lower Emotional Quotient

Kids indulging in the digital world and parents busy with their career have meant a social disconnect for most of them. People do not travel to their hometown or even to their friend's place in the same city quite often these days, often due to paucity of time.

Hence, kids do not have enough social exposure. It is what experts call a digitally induced social disconnect. The social awareness is low among Gen Z. Added to this is some degree of emotional shielding of kids by parents. All this results in low emotional quotient. A study published by Professor Jean Twenge of San Diego State University and Professor Keith Campbell of the University of Georgia in the *Journal of Preventive Medicine* reports that just one hour of screen time in children and adolescents may make them less curious, with lower self-control and lower emotional stability. This in turn increases the risks of anxiety and depression. The study also found that nursery school children who used screens frequently were twice as likely to lose temper.

Sleep Disturbances

Sleep issues are becoming common among kids and adolescents. Overstimulation by the gadgets and by the digital world is keeping them awake more than they should. Poor sleep habits hamper brain development and cognitive skills. A look at the definition of sleep tells that 'Sleep is a naturally recurring state of mind and body, characterized by altered consciousness, relatively inhibited sensory activity, inhibition of nearly all voluntary muscles, and reduced interactions with surroundings.' This simple basic human activity is getting harder around the world. A good sound sleep is necessary to restore the immune, nervous, skeletal and muscular systems; these are vital processes that maintain mood, memory and cognitive function, and play a major role in the function of the endocrine and immune systems. Sleep habits of both adults and kids are bad. Global studies by Wakefit, Nielsen and the KJT Group on behalf of Philips; data drawn from UK's National Health Service; and data from US Centers for Disease Control and Prevention (CDC; cdc.gov) and from US Behavioral Risk Factor Surveillance System, all point to poor sleep habits of people around the world primarily induced by excessive screen time and stress. Sleep specialists have emphasized the need to stay away from screens before sleep. Screen time at night keeps one awake due to cognitive stimulation and sleep deprivation. The brain's electrical activity increases, and neurons are activated and prevent the brain from calming down into a peaceful state of sleep. The physical act of responding to a text or a video or an email increases tension in the body that then produces the stress hormone called cortisol, which is naturally aversive to sleep. Furthermore, the brain produces a hormone melatonin that regulates sleep–wake cycles. Too much light from video screens at bedtime affect melatonin production, confusing the body that one is not ready for sleep. In kids and adolescents, addiction to digital devices can play havoc with their sleep and stunt their development.

Impact on Behaviour

It took Mary Beth Foster a few days to notice, but it was undeniable: Her son's first words weren't 'goo goo'. Her 1-year-old was saying, 'Ok, Google', after hearing his parents say it over and over. When she realized that, Foster says, 'My husband thought I was nuts. Babies say "goo" all the time, right? Until he heard him mimic us talking at the Google Home in context.' [1]

This piece from a popular English daily may appear to be farfetched but it's not. I have interviewed so many parents who told me that they had observed their kids trying to finish their homework using digital assistants. While these tactics by kids appear to be quite a smart one, except for questions that require short concise answers, the use of voice assistants for homework does not seem to be encouraged by parents or teachers. Such a behaviour does not encourage critical thinking among kids, which is one of the purposes of academic pursuits. Besides, when kids know that they are speaking to a machine which is supposed to be a voice assailant to them, they often lose etiquette. There have been parents who

---

[1] https://www.livemint.com/Home-Page/LS40eClj6B8HKFRgr1HSiM/
One-yearolds-have-started-saying-OK-Google-as-theirfirst.html

told me that they needed to tell their kids to be politer to voice assistants while giving them commands. Often it is noticed that kids become so overwhelmed with what voice assistants have to offer that they become impatient and pushy with them. In one such instance, a child would give a command to play a song and as soon as the song would start playing, he would request for the next song, and this practice would repeat. Hence, no song would play in full. It took some time for parents in this case to train their child to be patient enough to listen to the song he had requested, before requesting for another.

Mobile and digital overexposure have created a slew of behavioural problems unheard of before.

Sleep Texting

Sleep texting is a new mobile behavioural problem among zeners. A study by Villanova Professor Elizabeth B. Dowdell in Pennsylvania has found that the habit of reaching for smartphone to text while still asleep and having no memory of doing it is a common technology trend. Professor Elizabeth found students intimately attached to their phone. They keep their phones next to them even while they are sleeping. Sleep texting is akin to sleep walking, but while sleep walking is induced from the body's internal signals, texting while sleeping is usually prompted by external sounds. It's the buzz, beep or tweet that makes the person automatically reach for the phone. That sound gives the person a sense of happiness. Often texts sent out in sleep turn out to be embarrassing for them later. In her survey, Professor Elizabeth found that most students who were in their teens slept with phones close to them, about a quarter reportedly sleep texted and among them close to 72 per cent did not remember what they had texted in their sleep. Sleep texting is linked with irregular sleep schedules, sleep deprivation and recreational drug usage. It is potentially harmful for students who need to be alert and well-rested for their studies.

Phubbing

If sleep texting is a behavioural issue related with smartphone overuse or misuse while sleeping, waking hours have their own share of behavioural problem. So much so that it has led to the coining of a new term for such kind of behaviour—phubbing. It is the modern-day word simply meaning snubbing someone else by ignoring them while using a phone in their presence. Snubbing using a phone—phubbing—that's how this term was coined. Phubbing is very common these days, and I can bet that each one of us have either phubbed someone else or have been phubbed, or both. Phubbing is an annoying behaviour—a result of smartphone addiction.

Everyone phubs these days and at every odd place possible. You find guests visiting your place phubbing you and at times guests find their hosts phubbing them. Annoying, isn't it? Then you have couples phubbing each other. Friends, married couples and dating couples sit next to each other and keep phubbing. People even phub at work. People phubbing at office or during a meeting is not very uncommon. People phub at home, cafes, social meetings, offices and where not. I have heard people phubbing even at funerals. Worse, one sees kids phubbing each other at home at parties in presence of other adults. At times parents keep talking to the child and the kid simply does not respond because he/she is glued to the smartphone playing games, chatting or simply watching a video. They are phubbing you! Phubbing is like a global epidemic, as much as smartphone addiction is! The new behavioural problem! Why is it a problem? Because it affects relationships as it breaks down conversation, cuts communication channels and makes people feel ignored not getting enough attention.

Watching the Watch

Smartwatches connected to a smartphone via Bluetooth have become the latest menace for examiners in schools and colleges to contain malpractices in examinations. Smartwatches worn by examinees inside examination rooms are now being called cheat watches. These are Bluetooth-based or digital memory-based watches available in the market. They can show notes, images or formulas saved in the memory, with just one tap on the screen. This is not to suggest that cheating in examination is only by using smart watches. Cheating in itself is a behaviour that needs larger behavioural intervention in kids who practise the same. However, what concerns most educators is the easy and cheap availability of such technology that lures more children into such behaviour, with some being involved just for the fun of it.

Cyberbullying

Cyberbullying is a reality of modern times that threatens all of us but more so the kids and adolescents. The menace that the Blue Whale Challenge caused all over the world is well known. Hundreds of kids took their own lives, leaving parents, teachers and lawmakers around the world in panic scurrying to find a solution to end this dangerous online suicidal game. It is said to have been developed by a Russian psychology student in 2013 who claimed that he invented the game with the intention of cleansing society, by pushing those individuals to commit suicide whom he deemed as having no value. Much like the act of 'beaching' that blue whales do on their own accord, for reasons that are yet to be known, the name of the game and the game itself follow the same logic. One of the biggest unsolved mysteries of the ocean is that why blue whales 'beach' themselves causing themselves to die. That student was later charged and convicted of inciting suicide of a minor.

However, for the time the game existed, it caused much harm. To understand how this game was one of the worst forms of cyberbullying in recent times, one must understand how this game worked. The game would last for a total of 50 days, present-ing the player with 'daily tasks'. The game propagated itself via social media platforms. The game would start out between the 'administrator' and the 'participant' or the victim. Every day the administrator would give a set of easy tasks to complete. It would start with tasks such as listening to a genre of music and watching a horror movie clip. As the days progress, the tasks would become tougher, with one such tasks being to carve out a blue whale symbol on one's hand by mutilating the skin. The victims did these tasks because the administrator would threaten them with dire consequences if they refused to complete the tasks. Threats would include leaking something sensitive about the participant like a video or something or causing harm to the near and dear ones of the participant. The final task and end to the game would be to commit suicide.

Much similar to the Blue Whale Challenge, the news about a similar suicidal online game called the Momo Challenge started doing the rounds, leaving parents gasping for the safety of their children. The news fuelled the already heightened fears of cyber-bullying. Few teen suicides were linked to the Momo Challenge that supposedly uses the image of a horror artwork called Mother Bird by Link Factory to induce curiosity among children, challenging them to communicate with an unknown number. If a user refuses to follow the orders, Momo threatens them with violent images. While the Blue Whale Challenge was a terrible reality, news about the Momo Challenge was found to be a malicious hoax.

The terror of parenting in the age of social media and YouTube is nothing compared to erstwhile parenting challenges. Threats loom large in the cyber world, and the kids and adolescents become easiest targets of such cyberbullying. Even a hoax such as the one about the Momo Challenge can send the parents in a tizzy. The malicious agents of the cyber world keep an eagle's eye on the social media activity and posts of the young users and select their target keeping their eyes on the most vulnerable ones. Professor Artemis Tsitsika from the Athens University, Greece, and her co-workers undertook a school-based study across countries to understand the threat of cyberbullying better. Anonymous questionnaires about Internet use, social factor and cyberbullying were completed by over 12,000 students aged between fourteen and seventeen years. The researchers found a high percentage of children bullied online. They also found that teenagers who spend more than two hours a day browsing through social media without monitoring or digital literacy background may be more at risk of cyberbullying, often encountering electronic communication of an intimidating or threatening nature. The study becomes even more significant in the light of another set of findings that indicate the use of persuasive, at times even manipulative, techniques used by various digital online platforms to retain attention of users and keep them on their platforms for longer. On my smartphone, for instance, I get gaming app suggestions daily, despite the fact that I am not interested in them. Video-sharing sites pop up video suggestions persuading the user to watch a particular video, and other social media platforms make similar efforts to retain user attention. The aim is to expose users to partner advertisements and understand their habits. Behavioural scientist B. J. Fogg has coined a word 'captology' to describe the invisible ways in which technology can persuade and influence those using it. When zeners are exposed to this phenomenon of 'captology', they find their attention continuously being grabbed by the digital platform, making them stay longer and longer. User Experience designer Harry Brignull describes such interactions as dark patterns, defining them as interfaces that have been crafted to trick users into doing things that they may not have wanted to do.

Even adults are susceptible to such online manipulations. In a shocking incident, touchscreen technology meant to streamline school attendance in a school in India ran into a bizarre snag after it started popping up pornographic pictures on the landing screen. Tablets handed out to the government school teachers in Chhattisgarh supposedly got infected by a virus, possibly when a staff clicked on a spam or a porn site. Teachers from across the state are complaining about it and refusing to use the tablet for obvious reasons. If adults, that too educators, can be manipulated in this manner, I shudder to imagine the kind of manipulation the kids can be exposed to if they spend unguided, unmonitored time on online platforms.

Very recently in India, the TikTok app was banned for two weeks. It is a video-sharing application that amassed more than 120 million users in a very short period. However, the app was banned after an Indian court ruled that it could expose children to sexual predators, pornographic content and cyberbullying. The app was accused of provoking minors to post inappropriate videos of themselves on the platform. TikTok appealed the decision, saying it had cracked down on inappropriate content, and the court reversed its ruling.

Despite the reversal of the ruling, the concern remains, amid reports of online abuse of kids on the rise. In India alone, the cases reported of online abuse of kids have seen a threefold jump in 2017–2018. These cases include videos with child sexual abuse material, corporal punishment depictions, pornography and stalking. In a typical case reported in a popular English daily, a teenage girl from Varanasi called the child helpline number and reported that her cousin had created a fake account on social media platform using her name and mobile number. Further, her cousin had posted obscene messages and photos, resulting in calls from unknown people.

Digital Discipline

A popular missionary school in Bengaluru has introduced the practice of 'Digital Detox Day'. Every first Monday of the month, students of this school are off their mobile phones, tablets, computers and other gadgets. The Wi-Fi and school Internet are also switched off on that day. Students who have no phone or gadgets on that day and those who report misuse of gadgets are rewarded. Any misuse of the Internet, cyberbullying or creation of fake social media accounts is punished. In case a parent reports misuse of phone or gadget, it may be deposited in school for a certain period of time.

The boons of the digital world cannot be refuted, neither can be the fact that we cannot do without digital devices and technologies. We use many of them in our day-to-day life to make our lives easier, and in many ways digital is an integral part of our lives. However, digital discipline is necessary to ensure that usage of such technologies or gadgets does not reach a point of addiction and start impacting us in a negative way. Parents play a very critical role in many ways in inculcating digital discipline in their children. When to use, how to use, what to use, how much to use and where to use the smartphones, gadgets and digital platforms have to be taught by parents. This is what digital discipline means in real terms. However, parents must practise what they preach.

Time is a critical factor in implementing digital discipline— the time that parents spend with their kids. Both Dr Girish and Dr Anil feel that when couples plan their babies, they should also plan the time they will spend with their child after he/she is born. Dr Girish adds,

It's all about adjusting priorities in life. Some parents ask that shouldn't they have their own 'me' time. What is the definition of this 'me' time? Once you are a parent, the time that you spend with your child is also included in your 'me' time. The responsibility lies with both the parents.

Dr Girish preaches what he practises. Although Dr Girish is parent to a millennial, what he and his better half have practised over the past more than 15 years is exemplary and something that all parents should draw inspiration from. Dr Girish and his wife Dr Sumana are both paediatricians and busy. They however consciously took a decision once they became parents, that is, at least one of the parents must be at home with the kid every day. Hence, during the evening hours, Dr Girish and Dr Sumana practise on alternate days, each doing it for three days a week. Dr Anil adds how Dr Girish and Dr Sumana are revered in the doctor's community for being so disciplined with the time that they decided to spend with their kid, balancing both professional and personal life demands as equal responsible partners.

Dr Girish adds,

I find most doctors practising up to 10:30 or 11:00 in the night. It is completely about your life priorities and work philosophy. It is not like I will change the world by practising every day and so late. Yes, we might have lost few patients and may have earned lesser than our counterparts but then when we see our daughter academically and socially adept, we both draw immense satisfaction out of that and feel that we have done right. Some of my doctor friends want to work intensely for 20 years and then retire. I would rather work steadily for 50 years and live a life having balanced priorities and having addressed each one of them at the right time. What will I do after retirement? I will still be practising when I am in my seventies. This is because I have not 'burnt' myself in the past 15 years. Because we are doctors you would perhaps expect us take good care of ourselves. But then you will be surprised to learn that two of my colleagues in their early fifties died out of cardiac arrest very recently.

Listening to these two doctors I am reminded of a quote that goes something like this: We all know how to make a living, but we seldom know how to live a life.

Dr Anil, who is father to two zeners aged six and three years, says,

There is a kind of sensory deprivation as kids do not spend enough time with their parents. They talk to the mobile, they share their day with the mobile, eat with the mobile and sleep with the mobile. As a parent, I try not to repeat the same mistakes which I encounter as a paediatrician what most parents are committing. Like Dr Girish, I also try to spend enough quality time with my kids. Only when we set out limits can we as parents set limits for our children, the time that they spend with gadgets.

SMS: Social Media Sabbatical

Jhilik, a millennial in her mid-thirties and mother to a 'zener'—a three-year-old boy—is 'SMS'ing these days. SMS is not the usual messaging service or a new app. This is her own self-imposed 'social media sabbatical' (SMS). By her own admission, she was addicted to her phone. A homemaker since the birth of her child, she restricts her access to her phone by keeping it away from her hands but within her earshot to answer phone calls. She is happy with this break from her phone and social media. She says,

FB and WhatsApp had become huge distractions for me and I spent considerable time checking the notifications or updates that had little or no relevance in my life. Every now and then, I would check my phone and almost subconsciously my attention would go towards these social media apps. At times, something funny may be going around in group chats; I was responding to them. Later, I used to realize how much time I had wasted in useless chats. Frankly, with this break, my mental peace has come back.

Jhilik feels more mindfulness post 'SMS'. The phone would keep her busy for nothing and in this confusion, she would often forget her important tasks. She says,

Many a time this happened that I picked up the phone to send a message to Kanab (her husband) but when I opened WhatsApp I saw other messages, mostly in group chats. Forgetting about what I was supposed to write to Kanab, I started responding to those chats. After about half an hour when I remembered that I had not messaged Kanab, I picked up

the phone again to write to him and found that the four–five people to whom I had written earlier had responded. Once again, forgetting about messaging Kanab, I started responding to those chats. In the process, I would often forget writing an important message to my husband. He comes back at about 7 in the evening and only by 6:45 I would finally message him about essentials to be picked up from the store. This last-minute scramble would often be troublesome.

My phone used to retire to bed with me and leave the same with me in the morning, often waking me up before that with its notifications. But now things are different. I do not think about my phone till about noon when I need to make a few calls.

Jhilik also feels that she can give more time to her son post this break.

Earlier even when I would be feeding him, I would feel a compulsive need to check my phone updates. Sometimes, I would rush him up so that I could get back to my phone. All that is gone now. I am also able to play with him now.

Like yesterday, her three-year-old son Ritayaan wanted her to lift her hand; he would shoot with his toy gun and the hand was supposed to fall down. Earlier she had no patience or time for these 'games'. But now she can peacefully devote her time to the developmental needs of her child.

Ritayaan is using the phone less these days. Both Jhilik and Kanab were a bit concerned the way their son was modelling himself on their lines in terms of phone usage at such a young age. Cartoons and games were in an endless loop. Jhilik adds,

Two things have happened. One because I am using phone much lesser, I can tell him how doctor uncle has said that too much usage of phone can spoil eyes. He is listening to me. Else he had started to answer back and tell me that I am also using the phone all day, then why couldn't he do the same. I used to be speechless at such times. Even when Kanab gets back from office and is on the phone, Ritayaan tells him, 'Papa, do not use phone.' When such a small child is telling this to us and if we do not listen, then tomorrow he will also do the same. In fact, when we used to give him a choice between watching a cartoon indoors and playing with his toddler friends outdoors, he would opt for watching cartoons. It was becoming worrisome for us. Second, because I am using the phone less, I am completing all my chores in time and can take him for play outdoors during the evening. He normally gets tired because of all this play and eats his dinner and goes to sleep early. The whole cycle has become normal and hence mobile usage by Ritayaan has dropped considerably.

Talking about parents being role models for their kids, there could not be a better example, I believe.

Jhilik has got rid of her FOMO, a typical digital behaviour that has emerged in recent times. She feels that she is not missing out on anything important. Those who are close to her and at the same time important know about her 'break' and call her if they have to communicate something to her. Although she accepts that she misses out some interesting things shared on WhatsApp, Kanab being on social media helps her to catch up with those if she wants. However, she also feels that she has not missed anything that was critical. She also wonders if she would have been able to take this break had she been working outside her home. The second one does not seem to hold either as being a homemaker and a mother she has her hands full. It is not that she was or is free just because she is at home.

She is now planning to make creative videos like DIY ones with her friend and post them on YouTube. Creative, constructive and controlled usage of phone and social media helps one to discover the power of technology and channelize it in the right way. Jhilik signs off by saying, 'If I must be addicted, I will be with life not with my phone.' And we all have a good hearty laugh.

Dr Jenny Radesky of the University of Michigan in Ann Arbor, a developmental paediatrician, has found out in her own research that parents who are absorbed with and distracted by their mobile devices tend to have less parent–child interaction, have more conflict with their kids and encounter more difficult child behaviours over time. Parents who watch more TV have kids who watch more TV; ditto with phones as well.

Clearly stating the do's and don'ts of smartphone usage is important. Often, as I have said before, we parents are so distracted by our phones, so undisciplined ourselves, that not only we seldom think of such digital norms but also often lose the moral right to enforce such norms on our children, owing to our digital behaviours. Peter Harzheim of the German Federation of Swimming Pool Supervisors brought to the notice of the world how parents are risking the safety of their children at the cost of their smartphones. Peter brought to light what most swimming supervisors are experiencing. Parents become busy with their phones once they leave their kids in the pool. They are looking neither to the left nor to the right and certainly not at their children anymore. They are only looking at their smartphones. With high number of drowning deaths in Germany linked to careless swimming and cases of child drowning in the pool due to a smartphone-distracted parent underline the seriousness of the problem.

According to Dr Radesky,

With mobile devices, parents have a personalized interactive computer containing all of their work, social, informational and entertainment lives in their pockets. Parents must step back and think about their relationship with their phone. Instead of using it as a stress reliever, take deep breaths and go for a walk. Instead of withdrawing into a phone to avoid difficult family interactions, purposefully engage with others and potentially confront issues. Instead of losing track of time, be aware of attention hogs and notice how much time has passed when checking email or social media.

Jhilik seems to have done exactly what Dr Radesky has recommended, although she is unaware of such research. I am sure more parents can follow suit. One such practice that we have in our home is not using smartphones at the dining table. Not only my son but also my wife and I do not have permission to check our phone notifications while having a meal. Only urgent calls are answered.

Monitoring, supervising and guiding children's social media activity are important because online predators are at large threatening to annihilate the unsuspecting children and gullible adolescents leading to their nemesis. Even if it may sound as an interference, for the welfare of the child, it is important to keep a close eye on their Instagram invites/chat invites, trolling that they may be facing online, privacy settings of their account, profile views and invites from strangers and, finally, their social media activity. Any hashtags such as #bluewhalechallenge, #curatorfindme and #i_am_whale may be signs that the child is playing the Blue Whale Challenge, for instance. Psychologists also suggest keeping an eye on the behavioural changes of the children. During the Blue Whale Challenge days, teens who were swamped by the game wore long-sleeved loose-fitting clothes (to conceal self-harm), had mood swings, displayed suicidal tendencies and/or were constantly talking about death.

Digital discipline is a way to teach the zeners to differentiate between necessary and unnecessary screen time, desirable and undesirable digital behaviours, and learning to self-regulate digital usage and attain a balance between the digital and the physical worlds. Use of mobile for feeding the child, rewarding the child, ignoring the child and keeping the child busy often lead to long hours of gaming and watching videos, which qualify as excessive and unnecessary screen time. This can be easily avoided by guidance from parents. It is important for parents to be non-judgemental in their approach, having openness in discussion with zeners, building trust and using rewards to encourage positive reinforcement of digital discipline.

Dr Savitha, an eye specialist, feels that kids restricted by parents to use mobile often do it while hiding from their parents—in dark rooms, under the bedsheet, etc. Often, the minimum distance between mobile and eyes is not maintained under such circumstances. Parents should teach their children on healthy use of mobile and other digital gadgets—using mobile in a well-lit room, with the right contrast, and maintaining a minimum distance between eyes and mobile while using the same.

Dr Girish and Dr Anil observe how advancement in medical science has conquered infections and trauma among kids. However, at the same time, lifestyle diseases are on the rise induced primarily by the overstimulated digital world. Dr Girish adds,

Digital has its own sets of advantages for this generation of kids which we never had. They are well-equipped with information and have excellent problem-solving skills. However, problems arise because parents cannot set the limits when it comes to mobile and digital usage. At times, they are too busy to do that and at other times they themselves are guilty of indulging into too much mobile and digital usage.

The lack of balance in use of mobile technology and the early habit inculcated by parents play a big role in preventing addiction to mobile or gadgets.

Stuck Like Glue

Mishka is a three-year-old girl and only child to Mary and Tony. She is what you call a complete phone addict. She uses either parent's phone to play games, watch videos, take pictures, talk to her friends all day. She even uses the phone during bedtime. The only time she does not get to use her phone is when she goes to her playschool for a couple of hours. Her mobile habits concern her parents but whenever they try to take the mobile phone away from her, she becomes irritable and cranky. During these days, her parents attended a talk by Dr Manoj Kumar Sharma at their daughter's school. After listening to Dr Sharma, Mary and Tony were convinced about two things—one that their daughter bordered on the lines of mobile addiction and second that such addiction at such a young age could cause a variety of problems for their daughter. The very same day, the mobile was completely withdrawn from Mishka. She cried, screamed and even threw things on the floor but the mobile was not given to her. But over the period of next two days, her behaviour went out of control. She even threatened to leave the home if the mobile was not given to her. Alarmed at their daughter's reaction, Mary and Tony rushed to the SHUT Clinic of Dr Sharma to seek advice.

Aces up the Sleeve

Prevention is the best medicine, and ensuring digital discipline is a way to prevent addiction. However, if things have already reached a bad state, as in Mishka's case, then de-addiction is the only solution. Dr Sharma suggests a 'AAA' approach—acknowledgement, action and alternative for mobile de-addiction or pretty much de-addiction to any other electronic gadget and/or gaming/social media.

Acknowledgement

Acknowledging is the first step towards de-addiction—acknowledgement that yes, one is using the mobile or technology way too much and has reached a state where it is uncontrollable and detrimental at the same time. The process of acknowledgement starts with awareness of what defines addiction and how it can be detrimental in many ways. In the case of children, parents have a role in helping the child become aware of the hazards of overuse of the mobile. The awareness has to move to a stage of acceptance and acceptance has to gradually shift to awakening where there is an enhanced consciousness about excessive use of the mobile.

Action

Now it is time for action or in other words beginning of taking baby steps towards lesser and less compulsive use of the mobile phone. It can start with the introduction of the concept of break during prolonged mobile usage. Asking the child not to use the mobile can initially elicit sharp and undesirable responses. However, the child settles in this concept of break rather easily, according to Dr Manoj Sharma.

Another important action includes regulating sleeping time of children and ensuring that they do not use smartphones or any other electronic gadgets at least 30–40 minutes before sleep. Most children use phones before they go to sleep to relax. On the contrary, it suppresses the internal clock or circadian rhythm of the body, making it more difficult to fall asleep.

Know-Me

Wejdan, Zinab, Bayan, Kholood, Ghaida and Ameera are a group of young girls in Bahrain doing their undergraduate degree in business, who have invented a product 'Know-Me' to help kids get over their digital addiction. The objective of this product is not only to stop kids from overusing digital devices but also to engage them in other activities and at the same time facilitate human connection. Their mentor Dr Nehal rightly says that just stopping the kids from using the digital devices is not the solution. Whenever they are asked to stop using their gadgets, the moment they keep the gadgets away, they say that they are bored and the next question is: What will I do now? This dilemma of most parents became the idea for this product. The product looks like an ordinary board game but it isn't. It consists of a timer that sets time when kids would take a break from their gadget for about 30 minutes. The roll of a dice decides one card to be picked from three sets of differently coloured cards. Each card has a small activity that kids need to play with their parents or their families. The dynamic girl students of Royal University for Women aptly call their student company as Tech-Care (made to sound like take care). The ladies are readying the product to be commercialized soon as they formalize their company's registration. So soon you could also buy a Know-Me for your kids. It may not only help your kids to get over their digital obsession but also bring the family closer. Till such time, take care!!!

Other actions which help towards de-addiction from smartphones and digital devices include the following:

- Ensuring that no one uses any gadget on the dining table. The parents must first exercise this self-control before kids can be asked to emulate.

- Ensuring that there are regular family interactions and during those interactions no one uses mobiles.
- Introducing 'No TV Night'—one night take a break from TV and instead spend that time in pursuing a hobby or some other family activity together. If not, then anything like just having a plain discussion around each other's life also helps.

All these actions help to build self-control among children, and they slowly develop the power to say no to phone or other digital devices for some time every day.

Alternative
Developing alternatives to smartphone and digital devices is significant reinforcement of what I call digital discipline among children. Helping kids to pick up hobbies or pursuits other than those on their phones and digital gadgets is the final step towards de-addiction. These may include more of outdoor activities or other hobbies.

However, a very important point to remember at this stage is not to impose these hobbies on the kids. Instead, expose them to such pursuits or activities and allow them to organically pick their own choices and pursue them. And not to miss, all this works in phases. A sudden withdrawal of phones and other digital devices won't work. A slow-phased manner filling vacant spaces with alternative hobbies helps stack up digital and physical worlds best for the zeners.

Schools and teachers can also contribute in building digital discipline among zeners, but the role of parents is critical and non-substitutable. Together, we can help create a digital advantage for the zeners, rather than letting them succumb to digital diarrhoea.

5

TROUBLE IN PARADISE

———————

Arihant was always good in academics. But the moment he moved to the 9th grade, his father ensured that he had tuitions for his science and maths subjects. Arihant did not want the tuitions. He was confident that he could cope with his studies on his own, with a little help from his parents. But 80 per cent marks that Arihant scored in his first term exams were not enough for his father, who wanted him to score more than 90 per cent. After all, it was Arihant's father's dream for his son to get into the topmost engineering college of the country. Pressure from his teachers at school, his parents at home and to perform from his tuition teachers proved too much for him. The rote learning, unending hours of studying, expectations of his parents and the pressure led to a nervous breakdown. Arihant had to spend considerable time with a therapist and could not write his 10th grade board exams.

Manabi* (10) on the other hand is dealing with a completely different issue. For Manabi, it has been her fight with her body weight. She is dealing with weight issues and is tired of being teased and body-shamed in school, during play time in her gated community and even in public where people look at her and smile mockingly. Her weight gain was triggered by probably too much consumption of junk food. She has been trying hard for the past six months to lose weight, but her efforts have not yet been rewarded to a great extent. She is so exasperated that she now refuses to go to school or to public gatherings, even to step outdoors to play.

Mental health workers are reporting more and more cases involving kids and adolescents. Does it mean that mental health issues are on the rise compared to before? Consultant psychologists Ms Atashi Gupta from Kolkata and Ms Subhadra Gupta from Bengaluru agree with this fact. Both of them attribute rising mental health issues among kids and adolescents to a host of issues that we will discuss later in this chapter. However, Dr Roopesh B. N. of NIMHANS, Bengaluru, says that data may not be adequate to prove that such incidences have shown an increase among today's kids and adolescents. This is because of absence of comparative data of the past. However, he agrees with the fact that mental health is an area of concern among 'zeners'. Due to increase in awareness, lowering of social taboos and misconceptions about mental health, there has been a spike in the cases being reported and treated. The 2016 NIMHANS study points to the fact that mental health issues among zeners are on the rise. Whether they are clinically diagnosed or physically manifested; whether the incidence is greater in this generation or there is simply more reporting of its occurrence, anxiety and depression have come to occupy a greater presence in young lives. And this must concern all of us.

Other than anxiety and depression, mental health issues such as obsessive compulsive disorder (OCD), attention deficit hyperactivity disorder (ADHD), conduct disorder, specific learning disability and dissociative disorder are seen more in kids and adolescents.

Class Neutral

There is a widespread myth that such mental health issues among kids are prevalent among those belonging to affluent families. Mental health issues among zeners are common irrespective of the economic situation of the family. Take the tragic case of Indrani whose son Govindrajan killed himself after being denied a bike. Indrani, a widow who worked as a domestic help in Kizhkottaiyur village in Kancheepuram district of Tamil Nadu, found it difficult to accommodate the request of her elder son to buy a bike worth one and a half lakh rupees. She also turned down Govind's request to break the chit fund and use that money to buy him a bike as she had saved that money for his and his younger brother's education. When his repeated requests fell on deaf ears, Govind stopped eating and talking to his mother. Eventually, he took the extreme step and hanged himself to death. Unable to bear the grief of her son's death and holding herself responsible for the tragedy, she self-immolated herself on the day of her son's funeral.

Genesis

A study headed by Jean Twenge at San Diego State University shows that more than the realistic dangers and uncertainties in the larger world, the new generation is more prone to mental health issues because of their world view. The locus of control is an important factor and determines the likelihood of becoming anxious or depressed. It is the degree to which people believe that they have control over the outcome of events in their lives, as opposed to external forces beyond their control. The study clearly indicates the rise of externality and decline of internality when it comes to locus of control among the new generation members.

Something terrible might happen to me or my dear ones and I can hardly do anything about it or prevent it.

This perception of losing control is highly correlated with incidence of mental health problems among the zeners. The study further states the desire for material benefits and shrinkage of free playtime as other causes of worsening mental health among the Generation Z kids and adolescents.

Speaking to many experts on child and adolescent mental health, I could understand that there are other causes behind the deterioration of mental health of this generation.

Dr Roopesh provides a very interesting classification of sources of mental health issues: biological, psychological and sociocultural.

Biological

Biological factors of mental health issues are passed through genes from parents to kids. The transfer of these factors is seldom under control; however, the moderation and modelling of many such effects can definitely be influenced. Take for example characteristics such as poor temperament and low ability to adjust to new or changing environments. Kids with poor temperament react more than required, have frequent mood swings and hence find difficulty in adjustment. Dr Roopesh adds that such conditions require appropriate parenting. The child is already short-tempered, gets angry faster and if parents also behave in the same way, hit kids, then it is nothing short of a recipe for disaster. If such conditions stretch up to the adolescence and 'fire' is dealt with more 'fire', then at times they could become the trigger of teen suicides. Good and sensitive parenting is the only way to moderate and reduce negative genetic influences.

Psychological

Low self-esteem and poor self-image can often lead to cognitive distortions. Cognitive distortions are ways in which our mind convinces us of something that is not necessarily true. These imprecise thoughts are usually used to reinforce pessimism. Such cognitive beliefs end up telling ourselves things that appear to be rational and correct but in reality only serve to keep us feeling bad about ourselves, for instance, beliefs such as 'I have to be perfect' or 'I cannot make mistakes'; 'If I fail then I will fail in life, I will be a loser'; and 'One has to always succeed and for that one has to be always on toes'. Many a time, these distorted cognitive beliefs could be related to one's friends or relationships, for instance, 'If I lose one friend, then there is no meaning in living'; 'I have to be liked by everyone'; and 'I have to please everyone'. Such beliefs could also be about one's state of being, for instance, 'If I share my problem, then it equals to accepting defeat'; 'If I ask for help, then I will be seen as someone who is weak'; and 'I have to show a happy face always to the outside world'. Distorted cognitive beliefs about one's existence can also occur, for instance, 'If I am humiliated, then it is the end of life for me'; 'No one is suffering, other than me'; 'No one can understand my problem'; 'There is no hope for me'; 'I am helpless and hopeless'; and 'I am all alone'.

Filtering (mental filtering where a person sees only negative things), polarized thoughts ('If I do not succeed, then I am a complete failure'), overgeneralization (something unpleasant is taken as a norm forever), hasty conclusions ('She did not accept my proposal, which means I am not attractive to the opposite gender'), catastrophizing (what if a near or dear one is detected with a terminal illness), personalizing, blaming, fallacies (fallacy of fairness, fallacy of change, fallacy of fate/destiny)—these and more could be various types of distorted cognitive beliefs, often leading to anxiety, depression and other forms of mental health issues.

Sociocultural

The most basic and most important social unit in the world is family. Family plays a very important role in making or breaking a child's state of mental being. Often, dysfunctional families and flawed parenting could be the root cause of mental health among kids and adolescents. Busy parents, growing tension in their lives, child isolation, associated loneliness and emergence of gadget and technology as a sole companion of zeners are undoubtedly disturbing the basic social fabric of our society—the family—and affecting the mental health of zeners negatively.

Overcriticism, too much of disciplining, excessive and harsh punishments, failure to recognize the uniqueness in a child and forcing them to do or behave according to parental wish—in terms of career selection, choosing of hobbies, etc.—are all detrimental to a child's mental health. NIMHANS, which is one of the most renowned mental health institutes in the country and in the world, has seen a spurt of such cases.

'The most detrimental effect a parent can have on the children is when they tell kids, "Do as I say but do not do as I do". This is the worst example of parenting', adds Dr Roopesh. Preaching is not enough. When parents cannot practise it, they cannot expect their kids to follow their orders. For instance, if we are glued to our mobile phones most of the times, we cannot expect our zener kids to be doing any different. The new generation kids—zeners—will not listen just because it has been told by an authoritative figure, unlike the older generation kids for whom the words of authority figures like parents and teachers were the gospel truth. They will question and only a logical persuasion and lead-by-example approach will work with zeners. They are highly informed, aware and much more confident generation. They will never accept imposition.

Homes with parental issues like alcoholism, domestic violence or violence against kids are likely to produce dysfunctional kids with a spate of mental health issues.

The Hesitant Orator

'Cecil* came to me with a problem of stammering', recounts another consultant psychologist speaking on the condition of anonymity.

He was a teenager who had just stepped into pre-university college. During my initial discussion, I discovered that Cecil was academically very bright and had secured admission in one of the best colleges in the city. He had excellent written communication. However, he was getting 'stuck' in his viva voce examinations or oral presentations because of his stammering problem. Till his school he somehow managed but college was difficult due to strong emphasis on oral communication. His grades were getting affected and at the same time his self-confidence was ebbing. He was suffering from an acute inferiority complex; despite being immensely academically gifted, he felt he was not at all at par with the other students and did not perhaps deserve to study in such a renowned college.

Atashi Gupta, the consultant psychologist, states,

It took me about four sessions to determine whether Cecil's stammering was a biological issue or a psychological issue. At the end of the fourth session it became absolutely clear to me that this was a psychological issue and I started psychotherapy from the fifth session. Slowly I discovered his family background and his relationships—with  his family, friends and others. I could also understand that his relationship with his mom was strained, yet he was very sentimental about his mom. Deep within he wanted to be close to his mother, but something prevented him from being so. This needed deeper probing. Something, somewhere was not right.

The root of the problem went right to his childhood. Seven, yes, that's how young Cecil was, when he discovered that his mother was having an extramarital affair. This was the beginning of his stammering problem. Cecil could neither share with anyone what he had seen nor was it easy for him to accept the affair that his mom was having with his uncle and the way his father was being cheated by both. A storm raged in his young mind. He wanted to be close to his mother, but whenever he tried to do so, he remembered that sight and it discouraged him. His self-confidence was tattered and an identity crisis developed within him. He was unable to decide who he was? Was he a child of his father and mom, or was his uncle his real dad? Why were his mom and uncle cheating his innocent dad? Why was his mother having an extramarital affair? Did she not love 'dad' or him? Would she eventually leave both of them and go somewhere else to live with his uncle? Cecil fought with these questions alone. Obviously, he could never get answer to these questions.

Atashi adds,

It took me close to 19 sessions to complete the therapy and finally Cecil came out of his stammering problem. Till today he is in touch with me and is doing very well. Any sort of infidelity from the parents impacts kids the most, and they tend to withdraw into a shell, lose their self-confidence, and develop a serious identity crisis and self-doubt.

Seen Unseen

Subhadra recounts dealing with another very sensitive case. When she first met Andrew in a counselling session, she found him to be unusually quiet. Andrew had been referred by her teacher. He had been showing withdrawal symptoms, and his academic performance had also been dwindling. The child was not speaking up, and it was difficult to understand what the real issue was. She as a counsellor gave more space and time to the child for him to open up. It was during the third session that he finally showed signs of opening up. As the discussion progressed, she found him generally very curious about the physical relationship between a man and a woman. A little bit more of digging by the psychologist showed that the child was disturbed. Questions ranged from his sleeping habits to his relationship with his parents, his digital behaviour, use of laptop, etc. Finally, towards the end of the fourth session, he opened up and narrated the incident that had occurred.

It was a holiday for Andrew. His mother was working that day though. Andrew had gone out to play with his friends. His father was working from home. He finished play early and returned home. He was let in by the domestic help. He went straight to the study of his father on the first floor to tell him what happened on the playground that day. The door of the study was open and his father's back was towards the door. Andrew quietly stepped in with a plan to startle his dad. However, as he stepped in, he saw something unusual on his father's laptop. Andrew's father was watching a pornographic video. Andrew stood there quietly and watched while his father was oblivious to his child watching the same content standing behind  him. After a while, when his father was about to get up from his chair, Andrew tiptoed out of the study and hid behind the door. Once his father stepped out of the study and went downstairs, Andrew stepped in the study and opened the laptop. His father was careless enough not to close the window in which he was watching the porn video. Andrew watched the complete video on his own. After watching the same, he just put the lid of laptop down and sneaked out. The experience left him confused, unusually aroused, feeling strange inside as he was not able to understand or cope with the emotions and at the same time wondering why his dad was watching such a brazen content. He could not share this incident with anyone and slowly it started impacting him.

Andrew asked the psychologist what were the man and woman doing in the video and why were they doing 'abnormal' things to each other. Subhadra adds,

I am no one to sermonize adults whether they should or should not watch pornography but they should be very careful not to inadvertently expose their children to the same. Most porn videos are a distorted image of what sex is and are enough to ruin the future sexual life when they turn into adults. Worst, if a child finds out his parents watching such content, that to them is extremely abnormal as they interpret that to be the norm. The loss of image of the parents in the eyes of the child is natural outcome of such incidents and closes all channels of communication between them. In this case, Andrew was developing a feeling that his father was a criminal.

Most psychologists with whom I spoke had the same thing to say—it is time to examine the whole gamut of parenting in this age where adult relationships are changing in many ways and the digital age is throwing its own challenges. Both in Cecil's and Andrew's cases, parents had not only been callous, but they also set a very bad precedent for their children. Parents must lead by example and not do or say anything that might be inappropriate for those tender minds and against what they had been preaching their own kids.

If home is the basic social unit, schools for children are the next significant social unit. This is where they find meaning to their existence as kids, learn social behaviour and have their first brush with the outside world. Any sort of neglect or abuse in such environments is likely to scar the kids enormously. Bullying in school is another blow, something we will discuss later in this chapter. There are kids with learning disabilities, slow learners and those who need more time and attention to catch up with the rest of the lot. Such kids often find themselves at the receiving end, criticism and often humiliation from the teachers, followed by peer groups. They are often not included in group activities, leading to seclusion and isolation. Such kids are likely to become depressed and disillusioned, ultimately losing interest in academics and becoming very wary of people around them.

Society is the third and largest social unit where we all exist. Zeners are likely to be affected by the double standards of the society, gender-based stereotyping of tasks and roles and gender-based restrictions (separate dress code for girls, behavioural codes, etc.)

More Parental Factors

Excessive parental interference in the life of the kids can create trust issues between children and parents. This happens even more when the kids are growing up and becoming adolescents. However, in the case of zeners, these things can happen even in smaller kids. The kids powered with information in the digital age are far more independent than we think or let them be. While some controls may be necessary to augment for their lack of maturity and for their safety, excessive nagging, restrictions or rules can suffocate them and create nicety or depression in kids, often showing in the form of withdrawal or hyper-aggression.

The Party Pooper

It is Christmas evening. The streets are decorated with lights. There is a general sense of happiness with the New Year around the corner. Shops are illuminated. Sweet smell of plum cakes, Santa Claus dresses hanging from the store windows and stacked-up gifts are all common sights of the season. The chill in the air is not a deterrent for the party lovers. Young couples can be seen walking down the street arm-in-arm, lazily wandering about the decked-up streets. The twinkling sound of kids' laughter is difficult to miss and music is in the air. The mood is festive and that of a celebration.

However, this joyous milieu is not complimented by the heavy and serious state of affairs in Riya's house. Instead of jingle bells music, there is a clattering sound of falling objects and loud voices that are filled with rage. Riya is a fourteen-year-old teenager, whose relationship with her parents has not been the best since the past couple of years. The current crisis has to do with Riya's insistence

to go alone for the Christmas party at a club. She has not been able to get her parents' nod for the party that was planned to go on till late in the night. She was screaming, threatening to leave the house for the party without her parents' permission. On the other hand, her parents were also shouting and asking her to behave, pointing out her obstinate behaviour and trying to make her understand that it may not be safe for her to go to such parties alone. Riya's father even suggested that he can accompany her to the party and bring her back home after a couple of hours. Riya was rubbishing all such safety concerns. She was trying to tell her parents that she was grown-up enough to look after herself and that they should not interfere in her life. The anger was increasing and she was turning more violent. Finally, she locked herself in her room and one could hear her smashing her things on the floor. This continued for some time before it all fell silent. Riya's parents sat thinking how and when things started going haywire. Such violent behaviour from Riya was becoming all too common, especially when she was restrained from going alone out of the house. Her parents, more so her dad, had accompanied her whenever Riya went outside home since her childhood. However, as Riya stepped into her teens, this insistence by Riya's dad to accompany her to markets, parties, friend's place, her dance classes, her swimming classes—all of that was becoming problematic for Riya. She had often voiced her opposition for treating her like a child. Gradually, these voices became louder and then her behaviour turned more or less violent whenever such restrictions were applied on her.

Consultant psychologist Atashi Gupta says, 'Riya's problem is not an isolated one. This is often a confusion that develops in today's kids and adolescents, inflicted mostly by parents. At times they are told that they are grown-up and asked to be more responsible, do their chores themselves, behave and talk like grown-ups; and at other times they are admonished like kids, told not to talk or participate in adult discussions and often overpatronized. Thus, they develop a confusion whether they should behave as grown-ups or as kids. This often leads to identity issues. Maybe on Christmas eve, Riya's parents were right in not allowing her to go for the late night party, but the manner in which they were trying to convince Riya was absolutely wrong.'

Parents tell the growing kids that they must behave as adults, but they forget to define what it means. While parents mean behaving like grown-ups in terms of wisdom, taking responsibility, being more independent, and owning up one's action and implications of behaviour, kids many a time misunderstand and misinterpret that being asked to behave like adults means that they now have the freedom to engage in 'adult activities' and to enjoy the privileges that adults enjoy without really taking responsibility for the same. This is where the confusion starts. Parents often make such adult and kid comparisons based on their convenience, instead of teaching them that freedom without responsibility is not well deserved, becoming more independent does not necessarily mean endangering themselves, wisdom more than intelligence is developed through experience and how they should learn from social experiences. Riya is a victim of a similar identity issue and her violent behaviour is a sign of the confusion that she is experiencing within herself. Atashi adds,

Such identity issues are magnified among 'zeners' because of their situational aspects. The digital overexposure has meant that there is up-aging among today's kids. In other words, they age faster than their actual age. Adolescence sets in at the age of nine these days. Added to that, the shrinking size of the families has meant that there is either too much focus on the kids (as there are lesser family members and it leads to attention concentration) or parents these days have very little time for kids, leading to attention deficit. Not meaning to blame parents, but parenting by convenience is only going to add to such confusion that Riya is experiencing.

Perform or Perish?

Abnormally high performance expectation from kids can result in mental health issues. We live in a hypercompetitive world where most parents are concerned whether their child will be able to weather this competitive climate and make a place for themselves. These hyperconcerns of parents emanate from their own experiences, and they very unassumingly push their kids into this 'rat race'. Worse, they start comparing their child with their older or younger sibling or with other kids. Many teachers also start comparing kids with other students. This high pressure to perform, parental pressure and pressure from teachers and peers can often lead to nervous breakdown, disenchantment and severe depression.

Compar-i-Son

Kundan, a teenage boy and a student of the 9th grade, was not at all concentrating on his academics. His parents felt that he had no interest in studies. He spent most of his time in playing computer games or watching TV. His access to mobile was restricted, but whenever his parents came back home, he used to borrow their mobile and after that both of them were inseparable. Both of his grandmoms used to live in the neighbourhood and after coming back from school, every day, he would spend some time at their place till his parents came back from work. He lived with his parents and elder brother Sukumar.

Kundan and Sukumar studied in the same school. While Sukumar was a class topper and a school rank holder, Kundan's academic performance was dwindling. His poor scores became a matter of concern for his parents, so much so that they decided to change his school in the hope that new school would make a difference to his academic performance. He did well in his first examination in his new school. But after that, again his scores started dropping. The experiment had clearly not worked. Finally, his parents decided to take him for counselling.

'When Kundan was brought to me for the first time, he refused to speak,' says the consultant psychologist, 'He sat quietly in front of me with his parents prodding him to speak. But he just said that he had nothing to share.' Clearly, this was his way of giving it back to his parents. His revolt was a silent one and him not speaking was his way of making his parents fail in their attempt to improve his academic per-

formance. It took a couple of sessions for the psychologist to ensure Kundan opens-up and starts talking, which is a part of the therapy. It was then that he started opening up. His mother had been excellent in academics in her days. She expected both her sons to be academically brilliant and outperformers. His elder brother was an academic achiever. Although Kundan was also good, but Sukumar, his elder brother, always outperformed him and stood first in the class, something that Kundan found difficult to match. Kundan was constantly subjected to comparison with his elder brother, by teachers at school (as they initially studied in the same school) and at home by the parents, especially by his mother. Gradually, he developed a kind of anger against this comparison and against his elder brother. 'Why does Sukumar study so much? What does he want to prove? Why am I always compared to him?' These and similar questions tormented him.

His aggression increased with every passing day and slowly he developed a sort of allergy for studies. He revolted and decided that he would be completely the opposite of his brother. He lost interest in academics, and his academic performance started to worsen. 'It was a complicated reaction. Kundan, tired of constant comparison that he was subjected to and being made to understand that he was not as good as his brother, consciously and subconsciously set out to prove the same in anger and frustration,' adds the consultant psychologist Atashi.

When his school changed, his academic performance improved momentarily because now the comparisons at school stopped. In this new school, there was no more his elder brother, with whom his teachers would compare. However, this improvement in his performance was short-lived, as comparisons at home continued.

Academic performance in many ways is the single biggest defining factor for children, equivalent to an adult's profession, which provides them recognition and sense of achievement, fulfilment, joy and pride. Hence, with increasing performance expectation of parents and relentless comparisons, life gets really difficult for the kids, especially ones who have specific learning disabilities or who are slow or average learners who may be better in extracurricular activities.

Dr Roopesh puts it very correctly, 'No one tells them that it's OK to fail. Or for that matter that it is important to fail to learn.' The constant pressure to perform and show results that should tally with the abnormal expectations of the parents does them in. Dr Roopesh adds,

Most parents are not happy with 70 per cent anymore. Everyone expects their kids to secure 90 per cent or more. This may be back-breaking and nerve-racking for the kids. They do not recall their times. In their batch too someone got 90 per cent and someone got

50 or 60 per cent. But today, all of them are successful, all of them have a job, all of them are earning and all of them are happy. This wisdom is never learnt or remembered. That's where the problem lies. This illusion of a competition is nothing but a fallacy, and the parents pass it on to their kids.

Manjunath, founder of Mandya Chess Academy, FIDE instructor and a regular at the National Under-7 Chess Championship, has witnessed intense rivalry and the 'winner-takes-it-all' kind of attitude among kids every year. However, many kids are bogged down by parental expectation and pressure to win. He was quoted as saying, 'I have seen children who lose early refusing to leave the hall fearing that their parents would scold them or push them into instant refresher classes once they reach hotel rooms.'

Home 'Alone'

Domestic disharmony, abusive relationships and parental discord can take a toll on the mental health of kids. Occasional squabbles and disagreements are very common in most marriages, and they are not a great deal at all. However, more serious conflicts, hurling of abuses, name-calling, insults, long noisy fights and venomous interactions, threats of abandonment such as threatening to leave the house or divorce, parents physically assaulting each other, walking out from an argument, capitulation (giving into the other parent when there's not really a solution), withdrawal and long period of deliberate silence between parents create a stressful environment that creates a lot of anxiety and insecurity in the child. This can also affect the relationship between a child and a parent.

Domestic harmony in India has suffered more so in the past decade. There has been a significant increase in not only the divorce rates but even more in the number of couples who have chosen to remain separated. In countries like the USA and Sweden, nearly half of the marriages end up in divorce.

Researches have shown how sustained disharmony between parents can impact the mental health of children. A child from a very early age, as young as six months old, can exhibit distress when their parents fight. Fear, anger, anxiety and sadness may be various reactions of such children, and as they grown up witnessing incessant fights between their parents they *may 'externalize' their distress in the form of aggression, hostility, anti-social and non-compliant behaviour, delinquency and vandalism, or 'internalize' it in the form of depression, anxiety, withdrawal and dysphoria.*

Studies published in the *Journal of Child Development Studies* have shown that kids who face such parental fights show decreased cognitive development, inability to handle their own relationships often treating others with hostility, increase in behavioural problems, poor academic performance, decreased physical wellness, loss of appetite and poor nutrition. Adolescents coming from such families are more prone to substance abuse and have a negative outlook on life. A 2012 study published in the *Journal of Youth and Adolescence* found that children exposed to parental fighting are also more likely to have low self-esteem.

Child-related Factors

Child factors are mostly tech-driven today. The decline of free play time reduces social contact, and most of the social contact is via social media. Social media is the first media that allows many-to-many communication and hence can be a hugely complicated world for impressionable minds. The social contact now does not stop even after the kids enter their respective homes. Social media allows this social contact to continue virtually. This complicates things further as there is a sense of overexposure for today's kids, which is also detrimental.

Dr Roopesh feels that because of the way the world is today—hypercompetition with parents imposing their unfulfilled desires on kids—there is a gradual but definite shift towards extrinsic goals and decline in the belief that one can control one's fate. Such a scenario that prompts one towards material advancement and achievements, yet makes the person feel less control over his fate, can have an eroding effect on mental health.

Having said this, during my research and after speaking to an array of experts and countless people, I realized that most of the causal factors of mental health issues among zeners are parental factors and not child factors. I have to confess this and this further goes on to strengthen the belief that kids suffer the environment around them and the situations that they find themselves in.

However, two significant child-related factors need discussion. One is their inability to deal with the trauma of something terrible happening to a significant other and the second factor relates to relationship complexities among today's adolescents.

Fear for Dear

When something terrible happens to a near and dear one, the child finds it hardest to cope with it. During such times, empathetic communication plays a huge role. However, if their channels of communication are not open, they often find themselves claustrophobic.

Skyfall

Ritwik (14) was not coming to consultant psychologist Subhadra Gupta for the first time. She remembers counselling him a couple of years back when he was facing bullying issues in school. He was stressed. His academic performance had dipped to abyss, and his parents were very concerned. Counselling worked wonders for him at that time. She had counselled him, the rest of the class and also his parents and teachers to deal with the situation. Ritwik, who was flunking his papers at that time, was now one of the class toppers. Having known the power of counselling, his parents immediately knew whom to go to when they saw a change in his behaviour.

This time, however, the problem seemed much more serious and Ritwik seemed broken of sorts. Deeper probe revealed that Ritwik was very upset as one of his classmates had committed suicide. Gradually, Subhadra understood that the girl Srishti, who had killed herself, was much more than a mere classmate for Ritwik. He had a strong liking for her and when this girl took her life, the incident left Ritwik shattered. She decided to investigate the matter on her own before counselling Ritwik. She spoke not only to Ritwik but also to his teachers, friends and a few other people.

Ritwik and Srishti's parents were known to each other. Ritwik developed a fondness for Srishti but never told her directly. Srishti liked Ritwik, but she was attracted to another boy called Mohan, who earlier studied in the same school. Ritwik was not one of those obsessed types and quietly allowed Srishti the space while remaining good friends with her. Mohan, on the other hand, was very demanding. Srishti was an extremely well-behaved and attractive girl. She naturally attracted a lot of friends around her, something Mohan never liked. He didn't approve of Ritwik and Srishti's close friendship either. Mohan was intelligent and wayward at the same time. His waywardness was the reason that he was asked to leave the school by the principal and Mohan shifted to another school. This further irked Mohan as now Srishti was not always in his sight. Gradually, Mohan's behaviour turned negatively obsessive, and he started troubling Srishti. She unfortunately came from a quarrelsome family, and the frequent vociferous conflicts between her parents at home hardly left them with any time or energy to listen to what Srishti was going through. There were frequent conflicts at home and at times those conflicts were concerned with her choice of career or choice of friends. Srishti even witnessed domestic violence between her parents, and the situation only grew from bad to worse. With every passing day, Srishti went more and more into a shell of her own. Her change in behaviour was noticed by some teachers in her school. When it became too worrisome, they even summoned Srishti's parents and asked them to take professional help outside of the school for Srishti. It was unfortunately not taken seriously by Srishti's parents. Ritwik remained her only good friend during this whole episode. However, her communication with her boyfriend Mohan had become very infrequent. Mohan's threats to end his own life if Srishti did not meet his demands or befriended other boys had filled Srishti with a deep sense of fear and insecurity.

Subhadra Gupta says that parents have no clue how differently this generation of adolescents thinks compared to their parents, more so when under depression. Srishti was a part of many social media groups. One of such groups that she became member of was a scary one. This group preached suicide and propagated that giving up life is spiritual and that death can be pure. Ms Gupta believes that many 'zeners' become members of such social media groups and believe in the propaganda as they see the offline world to be too 'plastic' and artificial. The virtual world appears more real to them.

At a very later stage, Srishti was taken to a psychiatrist for help by her parents. She was put on medication and counselling sessions, but it was too little, too late. Only medication and counselling cannot work, until the environment around the person becomes positive. And the environment around Srishti continued to be negative and even poisoned at times. Many a time, it is the people around the affected person who need more counselling so that they can create that positive environment and become more empathetic by reflecting on their own behaviour.

As a result, Srishti's parents took her to Pondicherry for a short trip. But owing to their bad habit, Srishti's parents fought even in Pondicherry. Her father also had issues with her usage of phone and WhatsApp messages that she wrote to her friend Ritwik at times. So what was supposed to be a trip of bonding together as family and understanding each other turned out to be worse for Srishti. The last message that Ritwik received from Srishti was the one where she talked about how tired she had grown of life and ending the same seemed the only logical conclusion to her woes. Meanwhile, Mohan even visited Ritwik and abused and thrashed him. The very next day after they came back from Pondicherry, Srishti took the extreme step and took her own life by jumping from her apartment building.

This tragedy left Ritwik traumatized and heart broken. While in her suicide note Srishti did not blame anyone for her death, Ritwik knew that Srishti's life could have been saved.

Ritwik, more than anything else, needed a 'neutral' person to whom he could vent out everything. Subhadra informs that she did a deep catharsis with Ritwik, and the idea was to cleanse his mind and conscience of whatever he had gone through and give him space to cry. At that age, many boys think that it is not manly to cry. The timely support sought by Ritwik's parents, their support for him and later the kind of space provided by the psychologist where he had the freedom to move at his own pace for dealing with the tragedy made a huge difference to his mental state.

Subhadra refers to a recent incident when an aged person whom she and her family were very close to passed away and how she felt quite saddened by the incident, not being able to forget it, constantly feeling a sense of gloominess. At that time, few words from one of her friends who rationalized the death of the old man and told her that it was sometimes good to let go people who had died as it freed them from their sufferings made a huge difference to her state of mind. Similarly, Ritwik needed someone to hear out what he had gone through and to instill in him the courage to cry openly and gradually to let go and move on.

Ritwik could slide down the same path of despair and hopelessness had he not received timely help. Fortunately for him, he lived in a functional family and his parents sought help from a professional at the right time.

Status: 'Complicated'

The second major child-related factor relates to relationship issues. Dr Roopesh of NIMHANS adds that these days kids get into relationships early, triggered by cultural change, more exposure and awareness. Puberty among growing kids has also advanced, again because of several reasons such as better nutrition, eating a lot of packaged goods induced with preservatives, and social triggers such as movies and online content. Hence, the body is prepared for relationships earlier than before. Relationships with multiple partners are common, and love triangles are also common. Because of this, break-ups are also more often leading to confusion, heartbreaks and disappointments.

'Bermuda' Triangle

Abhishek's parents are worried about his behaviour of late. He has been absenting himself occasionally from school and his academic performance has dwindled. He is a student of the 11th grade and was known to be a good student, but when he failed in the chemistry paper during his mid-term examination, it shocked many, including his teachers and parents, although this was not completely unexpected as his teachers say,

Abhishek's academic performance has been going downhill since the past eight months. His concentration levels had worsened, and he was no more attentive in the class. He appears demotivated and has become quieter than before. He appeared to be crestfallen at something but did not share anything with anybody. He had also distanced himself from his friends and classmates. Something was not right.

Something was really not right with Abhishek. His teacher's suspicion was not off the mark. Juhi and Sameer were good friends of Abhishek and incidentally also his classmates. They had been friends for quite some time. But more recently, Abhishek started to develop a strong liking for Juhi and wanted to propose to her. The idea of having Juhi as his girlfriend was indeed very pleasant and appealing to Abhishek. However, he was hesitant. He suspected that Juhi liked Sameer more than she liked him. Over a period of time, Abhishek started developing a sort of inferiority complex. Sameer was good-looking and had a gym-fit body. Abhishek started feeling a bit outsmarted by Sameer. Added to this was a feeling that was becoming stronger within him that Juhi did not give him enough attention. He joined gym and started exercising regularly, hoping that a more toned body would make him physically more attractive and appealing. These techniques were not working out for Abhishek. His dejection and disappointment were growing day after day. Many a time he felt that life had no meaning and there was no sense in getting educated and working towards making a life when he could not have Juhi as his partner.

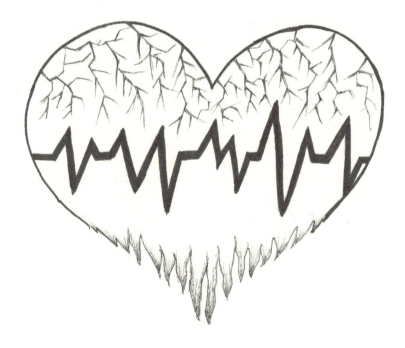

His behaviour towards Sameer was becoming stranger and weird day after day. Sameer was tolerating Abhishek's idiosyncrasies for quite some time, before one day both of them had a WhatsApp war. Angry messages were exchanged. Abhishek vent out his anger towards Sameer much more aggressively and made some comments that he should not have made. The result was disastrous. His friendship with Sameer broke and when Juhi came to know about Abhishek's behaviour, she also became angry and scolded Abhishek and stopped talking to him. This made things go from bad to worse for Abhishek. He felt a deep sense of emotional turmoil within him. Other than Juhi and Sameer, he had no good friend and now they were also gone. He had lost all hopes of impressing Juhi as she thought poorly of him as a person. It was difficult for him to share all this with his parents or with anybody else. Soon, Abhishek distanced himself from everyone and became lonelier. His parents tried to probe him about what was wrong. The only thing he told his parents after they nagged him a lot was that he felt no reason to stay alive. Abhishek had never made any attempt to end his life, but such words were enough to send a shiver down the spine of any parent. Abhishek's parents were in despair and did not know what to do.

Mental preparation for early relationship complexities does not seem to have grown at the same pace as much their puberty has advanced. The ones who go through it are often sad and depressed. Many of them are dealing with such things themselves, but in certain cases professional help is a must, feels the consultant psychologist.

Having spoken to a lot of zeners I realized that this generation is not frivolous about relationship; however, it may seem so. Most of them consider love and care as the pivot of such relationships and when they get into a relationship or try to get into one, they seriously want to see how it goes with a long-term perspective. It's not just for fun for most of them.

The fact that this generation is so serious about relationships makes them even more prone to mental health issues in case of these relationships not fructifying or in cases of relationship rupture. Their mind is not ready to deal with such issues, and we cannot blame them when even adults find relationship issues difficult to handle.

More Trouble

In one year (between April 2015 and March 2016), the child helpline number in India—1098—received 14 million calls for help.

Source: Mother NGO, CHILDLINE India Foundation.

There are significant number of 'silent calls'. Silent calls are those where background sounds are audible but the caller remains muted. These calls, experts say, are of greater concern as the distressed child may be too anxious or scared to speak up yet needs urgent help. The number of 'silent calls' has only increased in the past few years.

These stats are a clear indicator that there is more trouble brewing underneath and we need to look beyond just parental or child-related factors impacting the mental health of the zener kids and adolescents. The next chapter deals with 'outside influence' having a negative impact on the mental health of children.

Note: Names have been changed to protect the identities of the people and not cause any embarrassment to them or their families and friends.

6
DEVIL IN DISGUISE

In the previous chapter, we discussed parental and child-related factors triggering mental health issues among zeners and adolescents. This chapter examines the 'outside influence' in triggering such issues. The 'outside influence' includes all factors beyond the immediate home of the child. The parental role is however inseparable, considering that they form the first and most important reference and point of contact for the child. Frankly, it is extremely difficult to separately categorize these factors as they impact more in combination. The categorization is more from the sense of primary trigger and for the purpose of simplification in terms of understanding the issues at hand.

Contra-Band

Jahangir's parents were in a rude shock when they got a call from his school principal that he had been caught smoking cannabis in the school. He was in fact seen sharing the same with some other boys in his class. The matter was extremely serious and Jahangir's parents were summoned to school. Both being corporate honchos had little time for Jahangir. However, they left no stone unturned to ensure that he went to the best school in town and had the best facilities and resources available along with all the comforts and luxuries.

They both took half-day leave from their respective offices and were driving down together towards his school. It was really after a long time that they were taking a drive together. However, instead of feeling good about it, both Mrs and Mr Mustafa were crestfallen and worried. The multiple folds of skin on their forehead and strained eyes did not deceive their inner feelings. It was one of the most stressful drives that they had ever taken.

On reaching the school, they found Jahangir waiting outside the principal's office. He avoided eye contact with them and for the first time they noticed that their son looked terribly sick. Principal Fr Lewis met them, and it seemed that Jahangir had confessed to have started this addiction from a music band that he had joined about nine months back. They had induced him into smoking cannabis, promising him that it would improve his creativity. They made him believe that after smoking cannabis he would go into a state of trance, feel that he was floating in the air and that was the best time for creative juices to flow. Jahangir's parents recalled how he was always fascinated by music and wanted to become a musician. However, the Mustafas wanted their son to study and become a successful corporate mogul like them. Fear of being blocked by his parents to pursue his passion for music, Jahangir joined this band secretly. Unfortunately, his young age and lack of maturity led him to the wrong set of people. Everything from that day was a downhill, as Jahangir could never share his interactions with those band members, as his association with them was itself a secret. Fr Lewis was very compassionate and did not initiate any harsh disciplinary measure against Jahangir. He was very categorical when he said that it was not entirely Jahangir's fault. The rest unsaid was clearly understood by Mrs and Mr Mustafa.

On Fr Lewis's suggestion, Jahangir was taken to a doctor, who referred him to a de-addiction centre and also recommended intervention of a child psychiatrist who could help Jahangir mentally deal with his addiction. Mrs and Mr Mustafa only wished that their only child Jahangir would become his normal self once again. They knew that it was a tough road ahead and while Jahangir went through his de-addiction programme, they both had a lot to reflect and assess their role as parents. The Mustafas so very wished that they had done this thinking beforehand. But then realities were realities, after all.

The outside factors get magnified in situations where there was lack of open communication between the parent and the child. This may be due to the fact that both parents were very busy with their work. Unfortunately, this is becoming a common scenario in most homes. Dr Roopesh states it very categorically,

Only spending quality time is not enough. Quantum of time spent is also important. Parents cannot expect to come home at 10:30 PM and spend 30 minutes with the child and think that they have done their responsibility. No it is not enough.

The lack of communication between the child and the parents can also be due to an overstrict environment, where the child feels threatened to share his/her issues with parents, fearing con-sequences. Trust concerns can develop in the child due to various reasons, but the moment they find their parents inaccessible due to any reason, the communication at home breaks down providing leeway to 'outsiders' who can exert their influence, mostly negative, on the impressionable and gullible minds.

Jahangir is a victim of an outside negative influence, in this case, the band members, who influenced him to consume drugs. This is not an isolated case. Such cases of substance abuse are on the rise in zeners. An NGO survey in India revealed that almost 64 per cent of patients visiting de-addiction centres were introduced to drugs at a young age of below fifteen years. Heroin, opium, alcohol, cannabis and propoxyphene are the five most common substances abused by children. An emerging trend among zeners is the use of cocktail drugs through injection, often sharing needles. This also heightens the risk of HIV infection. However, overall, substance abuse leads to chronic depression and serious mental health issues among kids and adolescents.

Bruised by Abuse

Substance abuse is not the only outside influence. Zeners are extremely susceptible to sexual abuse and molestation outside their homes. Various agencies, governmental as well as non-governmental, have reported a spike in incidents of sexual abuse of kids involving educators or school staff. According to the *Washington Post* (2015), nearly a third of the educators convicted or accused of sexual misconduct with kids and adolescents had used social media to gain proximity to their respective victims. The story further showed that close to 80 per cent of children between the age of twelve and seventeen years had a cell phone to themselves and out of them close to 94 per cent had a Facebook account. This clearly shows the manner in which cell phones are handed over to children these days, how unmonitored and unguided their social media activities are and this definitely also indicates how uninvolved parents are with their children. Often, such distance results in sexual predators gaining easy access to children.

Such sexual misconduct with kids and adolescents is not limited to schools or only some predating educators. Often, the ones sexually abusing or molesting the children are the near relatives or close family friends and in some cases even members of the family, like in the case of Peenaz.

Violated

Atashi, consultant psychologist to a reputed private hospital in Kolkata, recalls the first time she saw Peenaz, an eleven-year-old girl, who had been admitted with symptoms of unexplained and sudden unconsciousness. Peenaz was lying in the hospital bed with her eyes closed. She looked pale and being so young, her face showed a strange kind of stress. Doctors had done all kinds of necessary tests and all reports were normal. There was nothing wrong with her physical health to cause sudden unconsciousness that Peenaz was experiencing. It was at this juncture that Peenaz had been referred to Ms Atashi, as the cause seemed to be psychological prima facie.

During her conversation with Peenaz's father Dhaval Joshi, Atashi discovered that Peenaz had a nine-year-old younger sister. Their mother no longer lived with them, as she married someone else after divorcing Dhaval. That was when Peenaz was just six years old.

Dhaval had a small leather factory and lived in Asansol. On questioning how he alone managed the two girls and his work, Dhaval told Atashi that his close friend Sumit helped him a lot. Sumit, according to Dhaval, was more than family to him, almost like a younger brother, who helped him in managing the girls as well as his factory. Nothing seemed unusual to Atashi except the fact that Dhaval's wife chose to abandon the girls while leaving Dhaval. Atashi thought that Dhaval's wife had every right to leave Dhaval if their marriage did not work, but how could a mother abandon two small girls just like that? Atashi also saw some scratch marks on the right hand of Peenaz.

Atashi patiently waited till Peenaz opened her eyes. Atashi tried to converse with Peenaz, but she just did not utter a word. Atashi tried to comfort Peenaz, but she stayed silent. Atashi knew that she had to be very patient with this small girl and it was also clear to her that something was seriously wrong with her. It was only in the fourth session that Peenaz started to cry and gradually opened up to Atashi. Peenaz had been molested by her uncle Sumit, whom her father considered as his younger brother. Sumit started molesting Peenaz two

years back. He used to pick up both the girls after the school, many times take them to his home, before dropping them to their house as Dhaval returned late from the factory. During these lonely hours, Sumit used to molest Peenaz and used to threaten her of scratching her with blade if she dared to share the same with her dad. Then one day, tired of her uncle's lewd behaviour, Peenaz lost her cool and threatened Sumit that she would tell her father everything Sumit did to her and all the 'dirty' things that he told her. Angered by this threat, Sumit scratched her hand with a blade. The marks that Atashi had observed on Peenaz's hand during her first meeting were from that injury inflicted by her uncle. Despite all this, Peenaz tried to tell her father about Sumit's behaviour but Dhaval did not entertain such complaints at all. On the contrary, he told Peenaz that she had lost her mind. Peenaz felt helpless and kept tolerating Sumit's tortures. However, three months back, when Sumit tried to molest her younger sister as well, Peenaz could not take all that anymore. With no one to go to for help and her sister also becoming a victim of her uncle's tyranny, she started showing symptoms of sudden senselessness. Peenaz broke down badly while telling all this to Atashi.

Later, when Atashi confronted Dhaval and told him all that his daughters had been going through, he was still not ready to believe that Sumit who was like a brother to him could engage in such action and behaviour. Atashi asked Dhaval clearly, who he believed more—his daughter or Sumit? Dhaval kept quiet. Atashi understood his dilemma and the state of shock that he was in knowing the true face of Sumit whom he considered more than family. Atashi asked Dhaval to quietly observe Sumit's behaviour for a few days after he went back to Kolhapur.

In the following weeks, Dhaval caught Sumit red-handed and handed him over to a police. Meanwhile, counselling continued for Peenaz and she started showing signs for recovery. Since she suffered from severe depression, Atashi had to refer her to a senior psychiatrist and with medication and counselling, Peenaz recovered completely. Peenaz's younger sister also had to take a couple of counselling sessions.

A UNICEF study conducted between 2005 and 2013 reported that 10 per cent of Indian girls experienced sexual violence when they were just ten–fourteen years old and 30 per cent when they were fifteen–nineteen years old. Nearly 42 per cent girls experienced the trauma of sexual abuse before they reached their teens. But such abuse is not limited to girls only. Boys also face the risk and onslaught of such abuses and violence. One of the first studies on sexual abuse of children done in India by Recovering and Healing from Incest, a Government of India NGO, reported 76 per cent of the participants having faced sexual abuse during their childhood or adolescence. The situation is not too different in other parts of the world. Studies conducted in Brazil, Mexico, Ethiopia, the USA, Croatia, China and other places show equally high incidences of vulnerability of kids and adolescents to sexual violence.

Children exposed to sexual violence are at a high risk of being susceptible to several other conditions such as alcohol consumption, illegal drug usage, development of mental disorders and spread of sexually transmitted diseases. Sexual abuse to a child can be grouped under having psychological, physical, behavioural and interpersonal effects.

Psychological effects include depression, low self-esteem, post-traumatic stress disorders, anxiety and panic disorders, guilt and anger, body image concerns and eating disorders, substance abuse, hindered cognitive and emotional development, hopelessness and suicidal tendencies.

Behavioural effects include law violation, little respect for social norms, poor academic performance, absenteeism from schools, abnormal sexual behaviours, violent behaviour and chances of them growing up as perpetrators themselves.

Interpersonal issues may reflect in the form of problems in communicating, insecure relationships, lack of trust and reduced social competence.

Other than these, grave physical effects are faced by kids and adolescents who are victims of sexual violence.

Prevalence of Various Forms of Child Sexual Abuse in India

Forms of Sexual Abuse	Prevalence (%)	Gender-Wise Distribution (%)	Dominant Perpetrator (%)	Not Disclosed (%)
Sexual assault	5.67	Boys: 54.4 Girls: 45.6	Uncle/ neighbour: 31	72.0
Forced to touch private parts	14.5	Boys: 58.4 Girls: 41.6	Friends: 38.5	77.0
Forced to exhibit private parts	12.6	Boys: 60.2 Girls: 39.8	Friends: 44.4	82.0
Photographed in nude	4.5	Boys: 52.0 Girls: 48.0	Friends, uncle and neighbour	71.4
Forcible kissing	21	Boys: 45.0 Girls: 55.0	Friends: 35.0	72.0
Forced to view private parts	17	Boys: 55.9 Girls: 44.1	Friends: 40.7	79.0
Pornographic material exposed to child	30.2	Boys: 67.0 Girls: 33.0	Friends: 66.0	80.0

Source: NCBI (2014).

A research study by a team of researchers at the University of British Columbia found that children subjected to abuse may carry the physical hallmark of their trauma in their cells. They examined the sperm cells of 34 adult men, some of whom had been victims of child abuse earlier. They found that the effects of the trauma were indelibly printed in 12 regions of the DNA of those men who had experienced varying levels of emotional, physical or sexual abuse. These alterations are called methylation.

The facts clearly show that most of the perpetrators are friends, near relatives or family members. Most such incidents occur or continue to happen unreported for a long time because of long hours of absence of parents or lack of open communication between parents and child or because of breakage of communication because of trust issues. Many such incidents are hence definitely preventable or can be detected at an early stage, limiting the effect on the child.

'Markup'

'I do not want my child to come back happy every day from school. Few days he should come back with some stress as well. There should be pressure of studies on him. Else he will not take academics seriously.' This is the statement of a mother of a two-and-a-half-year-old toddler, for whom she and her husband are scouting for a school. Even before the child has stepped into a playschool, even before he has learnt the first letter of the alphabet, even before he has even understood the meaning of a school, his mother seems to be contemplating a life ahead for him that will have only one benchmark of success—grades, grades and only grades.

This unfortunately is the case of most guardians in India. Somewhere we are transferring the pressures of the hypercompetitive world that we have built for ourselves onto our children. We are asking them to run in this 'race' of life even before they learn to walk properly—run as fast as possible and there is no other option but to win the race and then embark on the next race.

The pressure to perform academically starts before kindergarten classes. I remember a few years back when my son was studying in a playschool called KidzPark; after a few days, he started coming home with two homeworks to finish—one page of English alphabet writing and one page of writing numbers. For a child of three years who is still learning to hold the pencil properly, completing more than one homework per day was way too much and I did not want to put my son under so much stress. When I visited the playschool and spoke to the teacher and academic coordinator, they expressed their helplessness and told me that they did not want to overload the kids with so much work. But most parents who admit their children in their school expected that the playschool would prepare their child enough in one year to help them secure admission in a reputed international school next year. I told the coordinator that I do not have any such expectation and they could spare my child from this gruelling homework schedule. To my relief, my child was spared. But this is not the case with most kids. And in bigger schools, you cannot have a voice as well. This academic pressure reaches its delirium once the child reaches higher grades—9th and 11th grades, both pre-board years for the child in India. The moment kids move into these dreaded classes, the board exams start looming over their heads. A strange kind of fear psychosis grips most of them as they are subjected to a hyper-academic stress created by various stakeholders.

I call this a four-walled pressure chamber, squeezing these poor kids, as these walls keep moving inside, leaving little room for fresh air. The four walls are parents, school, teachers and society.

One of my ex-students, now working successfully as a marketing manager in a prominent real estate firm, told me the other day,

Sir, my parents moved me to the hostel right from class 6th so that I could score more marks. The hostel and school environment were very strict. We used to study for long hours but everything was for getting more marks. We never understood anything and hence I had little interest in what I studied. I had to just get good grades in my 10th and 12th grade board exams. I was told that my grades pretty much determined my chances of getting into a good university in India. After my school was over, I wanted to study business but my father wanted me to join an engineering course. I had to give in to my father's demands and I joined engineering. Again the same story. I studied with no interest and just for marks. Finally, when my father saw my performance in my engineering course, he let me join business studies during my master's programme. This is when for the first time I started really learning and marketing attracted me the most. I am now enjoying my career. I do not know why and what I studied, before my MBA. I feel it was such a waste. I wish I had studied my courses in school for developing an understanding and exploring new areas and not just for grades!

Sadly, this is the state of most of the kids in India.

The moment their child gets closer to board exams, the parents get into a hyperactive mode. They somehow take on themselves the responsibility of ensuring that their child secures top grades. Anything less than 95 per cent is unacceptable. The child is deluged with several tuitions from private tutors, arranged and sponsored by the parents. Even if the child feels that he/she can cope on his/her own, parents are restless and do not want to leave anything to chance. A regular day of a child suddenly changes and becomes ultra-busy—school, private tuitions, homework, self-study and no time to play or relax.

Study, study and more study! No wonder several start-ups have been created out of this frenzy of parents to get tutors' help for their kids. BYJU's, the online tutoring site for school students, has seen a dizzy rise in the past couple of years. Investors are bullish on the prospects of BYJU's, and today it is a Harvard Business School case study!

Most parents are very happy if the school where their child is studying has less activities, events and festivals and more and more of academics. Extra classes and extra assignments make parents feel happy and secure. The kids on the other hand keep getting crushed under this growing academic stress.

Recently, I heard a mother opining at a school open house, 'Mam, thanks to your extra classes and assignments, my child is very serious now. She wakes up at 4 AM and studies till late.' A child turning from being happy to serious concerns me, rather than filling me with delight.

The branding and prestige of a school are by the result it can produce with its 10th and 12th grade students, the number of toppers, the number of all-India rankers, the number of first classes with distinction, the number of first divisions, etc. Everything is loaded on results. The school instead should be recognized by the kind of teachers it has, the process of teaching–learning, the kind of fun that it can inculcate in learning and the amount of creativity it can fuel in the kids. But these are all traded in favour of marks. Schools cannot be blamed alone, as parents also build this pressure. But then schools in the era of competition have commodified education and the one that can get best results demands the best price!

Teaching is the art of making the less obvious obvious and the obvious look magical! Unfortunately, most teachers today approach teaching from a mechanistic perspective and the outcome of teaching is knowledge and not necessarily learning.

Knowing something is not necessarily understanding the same. Deep understanding of a concept or a theory is the basis for application, creation and innovation. The rote-based teaching practised by most teachers is focused on narrow outcomes of marks and grades, not on the broad principles of lifelong learning. Making students memorize things is not necessarily making them intelligent and wise. Wisdom and intelligence stem from how one sees learning in action.

Take for instance mathematics. Most students fear and detest maths not because something is inherently wrong with the subject, but because maths is taught in the most mundane method–problem format. In other words, tell the students the method and then make them do a couple of sums. That's it!

Recently, during an admission interview, I asked a student the practical application of the Pythagoras theorem. Although he knew the formula of the theorem, he could not tell me the application of the theorem. It had never been taught in his school.

That is where the problem really lies.

Hence, quantum overtakes quality. Outcomes are desirable in forms of marks. The pressure naturally is more on the students. The added pressure is because of the systemic disinterest for most subjects that is built in them through some really average teaching.

Finally, the society does its bit to build up the pressure on the kids. Society has two constituents with respect to education. First is the education boards that exist in our nation. These boards have generally followed a curriculum and propagated a pedagogy that is heavily loaded in favour of rote-based learning. Look at the CBSE reforms this year. All schools must follow NCERT books; all chapters must be covered in the year; students must be put through multiple weekly tests, periodic tests, pre-mid-term test, post-mid-term tests and more tests. Schools, under pressure to comply, are throwing out of the window activity-based learning, as such a huge syllabus and so many tests would leave very little time for activities. This will only intensify rote-based learning. We are bent on producing kids who look alike, do alike, behave alike but cannot think. It reminds me of Chaplin's *Modern Times.*

The second constituent is the society at large—a society that perceives a child good in mathematics as intelligent, and the one good in humanities as useless; one that perceives a child good in English as smart and suave, and the one who can speak a good regional language or Hindi as illiterate; one that looks down on and almost condemns children who fail to score too well. There is no place for ability; only one's grades can be a testimony to one's worth and nothing else.

I look at the poor child bent forward by the weight of his school bag, parent's expectations, school's and teacher's dictum, and society's 'high' benchmarks and worry how the education and the societal systems are killing creativity, stunting growth and dulling a curious mind.

Have we asked ourselves the following question?

Why do children stop asking questions as they grow up?

Why do kids not enjoy classes?

Why do they rejoice when a teacher does not turn up on a day in the school?

Why is the number of mental health cases such as anxiety and depression on the rise among kids?

Why is the number of kids killing themselves after failing to secure good grades on the rise?

Why do most kids say in admission interviews that they never got a chance to choose the desired field of study?

Why, as a nation that has 1.6 billion people, do we not have more patents and innovations in our name?

Why, despite having such highbrow schools and institutes of higher learning, do we produce more workers than thinkers?

Why, despite so much competition, do our kids end up with the same repetitive jobs?

Many such questions find no takers. And often defence is offered in various forms.

Students Kill Themselves for Grades

Kota in Rajasthan, India, is the personification of this obsession for marks. For most parents, an engineering seat in an Indian Institute of Technology (IIT) is the ultimate fantasy. Kota is home to thousands of coaching classes who prepare the aspirants for the competitive exams with a promise to help them crack the entrance and secure a seat for themselves. And every year many teenagers kill themselves unable to cope with the pressure to perform and the tonnage of parental and societal expectations. In 2016, the number of teenagers studying in various coaching institutes who killed themselves in Kota was 57. A nationwide sensation over the spate of suicides saw numbers dropping as coaching institutes and hostels kept a close eye on the students' behaviour; however, the inhuman mental stress continues. The suicide numbers also do not tell us about the others who suffer from severe anxiety, depression and nervous breakdown. The cost that parents bear (approx ₹600,000 for one child per annum), the heavily lopsided ratio of aspirants versus IIT seats, pressure from caching classes to build and protect their reputation, and societal and family expectations (for them it is a question of their family pride) become too much to handle for the poor teenager most of the times.

Interestingly, one of Britain's biggest graduate recruiters EY, a global accountancy firm, recently announced that it was scrapping the requirement for applicants to have a minimum 2:1 degree pass or UCAS Point score of 300 (the equivalent of three B grades at A level). This is part of the company's effort to attract millennial talent and hence open up opportunities for talented individuals regardless of their educational background and provide greater access to the profession.

Hook or Crook

Coercive schooling or corporal punishment is another reason for mental health issues in kids and adolescents. UNICEF's Committee on the Rights of the Child in the General Comment No. 8 defines 'corporal' or 'physical' punishment as

> any punishment in which physical force is used and intended to cause some degree of pain or discomfort, however light. Most involves hitting ('smacking', 'slapping', 'spanking') children, with the hand or with an implement…. In the view of the Committee, corporal punishment is invariably degrading. In addition, there are other non-physical forms of punishment that are also cruel and degrading and thus incompatible with the Convention. These include, for example, punishment which belittles, humiliates, denigrates, scapegoats, threatens, scares or ridicules the child.

Lock-Up

Keerthan studies in the 3rd grade in a private English-medium school run by a local influential family. Although the school has a principal, the de facto head of the school is a lady by the name of Rani, younger daughter of the promoter. Rani was known for high-handedness and for her abrasive behaviour. Teachers, staff and students are equally terrified of her. She was a despicable character in school, yet everyone had to tolerate her as she was from the promoter's family.

This case of an unofficial head of an academic institution from the promoter family is a common occurrence in India. And though everyone dislikes this character, with a value of 'fitting in', most people keep quiet and want to remain in the good books of this 'dictator'.

Most teachers and academic staff also tried to fit in, and reporting an incident to Rani was equivalent to earning 'brownie points'. Many teachers had also started following Rani and using corporal punishment freely on the students.

The table that Keerthan used using in his classroom had a chip coming off its corner owing to wear and tear. He had complained about the protruding chip of his table to his class teacher. However,

little was done to address the same. One day, after one of the classes, as Keerthan pulled up his bag to put books of his previous period back and take out the next one, his bag rubbed against the protruding chip and the wooden chip fell on the floor. This was interpreted by one of his teachers as Keerthan deliberately trying to damage school property. The word reached the primary coordinator and then to the vice-principal, who instead of checking with the class teacher for facts or dealing with the issue herself reported the matter to Rani. Keerthan was detained in school after school hours and Rani locked him up in her office as she sat outside turning a deaf ear to his wails and desperate screams. The school's principal whose office was within earshot stayed put in her office, caring more for saving her job than stopping this 'act'. Keerthan's parents were immediately summoned to the school. When his father arrived at the school, it was over 45 minutes that Keerthan had been locked in the office. When finally the door was opened at the request of Keerthan's father, he shot out of the office straight into his father's lap, screaming 'save me', 'save me', and the next moment he fainted in his father's arms.

Despite clear laws regarding banning all forms of corporal punishment in India, sadly the implementation on the ground is poor. Most Western countries have banned corporal punishment. The first state to ban corporal punishment in the USA was New Jersey in 1867.

In India, a law was introduced in the year 2000 banning corporal punishment. Later, even the Right of Children to Free and Compulsory Education Act (RTE Act) enacted in 2009 framed strong rules against corporal punishment. CBSE—one of the prime education boards in India—has issued strict guidelines to schools warning against use of any form of corporal punishment in schools. Notwithstanding all these laws, acts and guidelines, unfortunately corporal punishment is still rampantly used in schools; institutions meant for care and protection of children such as hostels, orphanages, ashram schools and juvenile homes; and even in the family setting.

School Anxiety

Rishi and Neha are having a tough time with their six-year-old son Aditya. He simply refuses to go to his new school. He starts crying at the faint mention of going to school. For the past week or so, Aditya, or Adi as his parents lovingly call him, does not want to leave either of his parents even for a minute. Rishi is on leave from his office for the past four days and has been extremely worried. The moment either Rishi or Neha is out of Adi's sight, he would start crying, while searching for them. For Rishi and Neha, even going to the bathroom has become difficult. Whenever they have to do so, Adi would go near the bathroom and bang the door, asking his dad or mom to come out, all this while crying inconsolably. A professional counsellor had visited them just a day back. She called it extreme school anxiety. This happens to kids who face negative, fear-inducing incidents in their school generally. In Adi's case, when he was transitioned from his neighbourhood Montessori playschool to a reputed international school in the city, all hell broke loose. Adi was naturally overwhelmed going from a small cosy school to a big international school with so many kids and teachers. Naturally, he cried on the first few days of his school.

But instead of managing him properly and making him feel comfortable in the new setting, his teacher reportedly locked him alone in the

classroom when he refused to stop crying. The school principal threatened to make him stay back after the school hours and make him clean the classroom floor if he did not listen to his teacher. There were also instances of school support staff dragging Adi by his hand or even threatening to hit him. All this was too much for the poor boy.

He was already dealing with the anxiety of stepping into this huge school, and such treatment at the hands of staff, teacher and principal made him completely phobic to school. The counsellor has recommended to pull Adi out of this new school, more counselling sessions for the child and parents, play therapy and gradually the transition of Adi to a better school. Rishi and Neha never imagined that their innocent little boy would have to deal with a mental health issue because of errors and blunders committed by the school staff.

69% of kids in India have faced corporal punishment in India

54.68% Boys

Every 2 out of 3 kids in India face corporal punishment in Schools

73% of the Boys

Corporal Punishment rampant in Homes

45.32% Girls

65% of the Girls

88.6% abused by Parents

Rest others

Sources: NCPCR, UNICEF.

Corporal punishments have been recognized by psychologists, law makers and educators to be degrading and having a huge negative impact on a child's mental health. Adverse effects of corporal punishment include direct physical harm, negative impacts on mental and physical health, poor moral internalization and increased antisocial behaviour, increased aggression in children, increased violent and criminal behaviour as they grow up as adults, damaged education and damaged family relationships.

Zeners or Generation Z kids are even more sensitive to the effects of corporal punishments as they have grown up in a far more volatile and uncertain environment. They are growing up in increasingly fragmented nuclear families with the advent of technology and time becoming a rare commodity. Being exposed to a greater turbulence and having less shock absorbers, degrading forms of correction and reinforcements like corporal punishment can scar a child mentally and psychologically forever.

A research study conducted by the University of Michigan revealed that children who are subjected to corporal punishment are more likely to suffer from depression and have suicidal tendencies in their later life. Last year, four boys committed suicide in Vellore district of Tamil Nadu after they were forced to hold their hands up in the air for over two hours, as the teachers hurled abuses at them, calling them dogs, buffaloes and 'worse than Mumbai dons' for their mistake. Data clearly suggest that such suicide incidents are not isolated ones.

Childhood Spanking and Mental Health		
55% respondents reported being spanked in childhood.	Men and Minority participants had experienced more spanking than women and white participants respectively.	Those exposed to spanking in childhood had more chances of suffering from mental health problems.

Source: Twitter @UMichiganNews, available at https://news.umich.edu/spanking-creates-defiant-aggressive-children/ (accessed on 22 Nov 2019).

The University of Michigan research also showed that those who are spanked when they are kids are more likely to grow up as adults who engage in substance abuse, alcoholism, and physical and emotional abuse. Hence, corporal punishments do not only have short-term damages, but they also scar a child forever. In kids, it starts with anxiety like school anxiety in the case of Aditya (the story above); if continued, older kids and adolescents develop depression and suicidal tendencies; and as they grow up as adults, many of them develop abnormal social behaviours. Children who face harsh corporal punishment have also been found to have reduced gray matter volume in the prefrontal cortex in brain, which is believed to play a strong role in social cognition.

Studies have revealed a strong positive correlation between good childhood memories and good health in young adults. In other words, happy children grow up as healthy adults. Children who have good childhood memories have higher quality of work life and personal relationships, lower substance abuse, and lower depression and health-related problems when they grow up as adults. Recently, the American Academy of Pediatrics issued a strongly worded policy warning parents and educators against the use of corporal punishment or any other non-physical punishment that is degrading or denigrating to the child. Experts strongly recommend the elimination of violence and fear in relationships.

Bull in a China Shop

Bullying is another serious threat faced by zener kids and adolescents. CDC reports that a high number of students have faced bullying and/or cyberbullying. Thirty-three per cent of all students aged between twelve and eighteen years have faced bullying. Twenty per cent of high-school students and twenty-five per cent of middle-school students have faced bullying at least once in their life. Bullying can have both short- and long-term negative effects on a child's mental and physical health.

The Broken 'Star'

'Why my son?' That's the only question that Sharmista kept repeating while inconsolably weeping for days and days after the death of her son Mridul (names changed). Sharmista was in a terrible state, and all efforts by her husband Tanmay to console her seemed to fail. Tanmay was also devastated by his son's death, but he somehow held himself together for the sake of his wife and their elder daughter Koel who was finishing her college. The past week had been distressing for all of them, and Mridul's suicide had shattered their otherwise beautiful family.

Tanmay worked in a reputed multinational company, while Sharmista was a teacher in a high school. Both their kids Koel and Mridul had always been very nice and understanding kids. Koel was older and more outspoken, while Mridul was the quieter one. They shared a good family bonding and were known to their neighbours as a peace-loving, educated, decent family. Neighbours were in a state of shock at Mridul taking this extreme step, and no one knew whom to really blame for his death or how to react to this tragedy. The past one week had been tough for Mridul's family not only because of his death but also because of the constant phone calls, police investigation and media attention. The turn of events had tormented them to the core and for Tanmay, Sharmista and Koel the air seemed thinner and breathing seemed a privilege.

Mridul was always the first one to get home in the afternoon, generally followed by Sharmista an hour later from her school, followed by Koel in the evening and Tanmay used to come back home much later, post 9 PM. That was the normal schedule for all of them. So when Mridul used to come back from his school, no one would be there at home. That fateful day, after Mridul got down from the bus, he did not go to his apartment. Instead, he went to the ninth floor of his building and jumped to his death.

What prompted Mridul to go to the ninth floor and not to his apartment like he normally used to do? What made him take this extreme step?

The media attention in this case was huge. In fact, Mridul's father had to even attend a local TV show on the growing number of suicides in adolescents with a special focus on Mridul's death. The intense media scrutiny and resulting public outcry on the case triggered a swift police investigation. Mridul's parents and sister had not detected anything hugely unusual except that Mridul had grown quieter in the past few months. Since Mridul had always been a shy and reserved child, his parents dismissed his recent behaviour as an adolescent trend. Koel also told police that Mridul had occasionally complained in the past few months that some of his seniors were troubling him in school and also in the bus. In fact, one day, about three months back, when Mridul came home very disturbed, then Tanmay had called up his class teacher and complained too. After this, all of them assumed that things had been set right as Mridul never spoke about the issue after that.

But the truth was far more than that. Mridul faced heavy bullying at school by his seniors. He was a simpleton, quiet and shy. The constant bullying, name-calling and at times even physical manhandling by his seniors were traumatizing for Mridul. This bullying continued in the bus. After Mridul's father complained to the teacher, instead of reducing, the bullying became even more intense and humiliating. Mridul used to be bullied in places where they were more out of sight when it came to teachers—like in restrooms or in the bus. The seniors bullying Mridul even threatened him of dire consequences if he ever again complained to anyone. Most other students, especially his classmates, had witnessed Mridul getting bullied by the seniors. Many of them were mute spectators or were just too scared to say anything. The teachers did scold the bullies once, but no one at school took it with the degree of seriousness with which it should have been taken. At home, Mridul was quiet because he was scared and he probably did not want to appear weak or trouble his parents with what was happening in the school. His parents mistook his silence as his adolescent behaviour and ignored it. Tanmay even admitted that he did not probe further as he thought Mridul would learn to deal with his issues and challenges himself and that would make him strong.

What probably no one understood was that in keeping things bottled up, Mridul was setting himself up for a disaster in waiting. And that's exactly what happened. On the fateful day, a line must have been crossed and that ended being the last straw for Mridul.

He must have got so fed up and upset that instead of going to his apartment, he went to the ninth floor of the same building and jumped to oblivion. The pain must have become too much for the poor child. Mridul was a kind of child who never blamed anyone. He had not left a suicide note behind, but one of his last poems that was later found in his notebook showed that something was troubling him deeply.

Bullying is a serious issue and can be very painful and cause high levels of anxiety and nervous breakdown among kids and adolescents. A change in behaviour in a child or adolescent must be immediately flagged, and parents must immediately take a professional counsellor or psychologist's help to help their child resolve the issues. No child becomes strong by adults ignoring such serious issue like bullying. Instead, they become strong by knowing how to deal with it. Just a scolding by the teacher is not enough to set things right.

Generation Z Attitude Survey Reveals Their Vulnerability

An attitude survey that I conducted among zeners showed that they had low tolerance to acceptance of physical aggression, verbal derogation and social exclusion. In other words, they would not accept physical aggression or verbal derogation being meted out to fellow zeners, nor would they accept social exclusion of anyone with whom they or others have a conflict. However, the same survey also revealed that when they are confronted with physical aggression, verbal derogation or social exclusion, they are not confused about their perceived social competence to deal with the same. Nearly half of them perceive themselves adept in dealing with such violence or exclusion and the other half perceive that they would find it hard to deal with such intimidations.

This makes two things very clear—they do not subscribe to the violence or social omission in dealing with conflicts but at the same time they do not know too well how to protect themselves from such behaviour from others and hence can be labelled as a vulnerable cohort. The survey involved a large number of participants who were surveyed over a period of more than one year.

Breaking the Camouflage

The discussions in the chapter clearly show that many times the greatest risk to our children emanates from someone we deeply trust or the ones we least expect it from. They may be friends, close relatives, complete strangers and at times even educators. This is not to create a sense of mistrust, rather to sensitize against blindly trusting anyone when it comes to children. The next chapter discusses in detail strategies to prevent and address mental health issues among zeners. The chapter also examines the role of parents and teachers—the two primary stakeholders in managing mental health.

References

NCPCR. (2018, September 7). NCPCR received over 5000 child abuse complaints in last 3 years. *The Times of India*. Retrieved 22 June, from https://timesofindia.indiatimes.com/india/ncpcr-received-over-5000-child-abuse-complaints-in-last-3-years/articleshow/65721038.cms

Singh, M. M., Parsekar, S. S., & Nair, S. N. (2014). An epidemiological overview of child sexual abuse. *Journal of Family Medicine and Family Care, Vol. 3*(Issue 4), 430–435. Retrieved from https://www.ncbi.nlm.nih.gov/pmc/articles/PMC4311357/

UNICEF. (2016, June). *Protecting children from online sexual exploitation.* UNICEF. Retrieved 22 Nov, from https://www.unicef.org/protection/

files/FBO_Guide_for_Religious_Leaders_and_Communities_ENG(1).
pdf

UNODC. (2015). *Study on the effects of new information technology on abuse and exploitation of children*. UNODC. Retrieved 22 Nov 2019, from https://www.unodc.org/documents/Cybercrime/Study_on_ the_Effects.pdf

Washington Post. (2019, October 25). 'I don't know about normal love': A church leader's abuse and a woman's years-long struggle. *Washington Post*. Retrieved 22 Nov 2019, from https://www.washingtonpost.com/ local/i-dont-know-about-normal-love-a-church-leaders-abuse-and-a-womans-years-long-struggle/2019/10/24/140dd2c2-f59f-11e9-a285-882a8e386a96_story.html

7

LIGHTHOUSE ON THE BEACH

Zeners are vulnerable to mental health issues far more than kids and adolescents of the previous generations. While the causal factors may not always be in our control, but most mental health issues can be prevented by timely intervention. While the two previous chapters focused on triggers inside and outside, or causal factors of mental health issues among zeners, this chapter discusses ways to prevent and address such mental health issues.

Warning Signs of Mental Health Issues

Any change from usual routine could be a warning sign of a deteriorating mental health among kids and adolescents. Any such sign should not be ignored by parents, and they should keep a close watch on their children. If these symptoms persist, they should communicate with the child and try to understand the issues bothering them. If these still persist, then it may be the time to call for professional help of a counsellor or a consultant psychologist. Symptoms include the following:

- Reduced talking
- Spending more time alone
- Irritability

- Unexplained anger
- Crying more often
- Avoiding friends
- Reduced interest in eating food
- Reduced sleep hours
- Losing interest in academics
- Falling academic performance
- Losing interest in going to school
- No interest in grooming oneself
- Reduced hygiene
- Diminished interest in online activities

Clear Signs of Mental Health Issues

Dr Roopesh says, 'While the above ones are warning signs, there may be certain clear signs that indicate that the kid or adolescent is definitely suffering from a mental health issue.' These include one or more of the following:

- Refusing to go to school
- Getting up late in the morning so as to avoid school
- Not able to go to sleep
- Refusing to take bath
- Crying easily and bitterly
- Sad mood, more often
- Talking about death
- Talking like 'It's better to be dead', 'What's the point in remaining alive?' etc.
- Not interacting with parents or siblings

Any such sign needs urgent attention, and it is better to immediately take a good professional help for the child. Subhadra says that although parents talk with all good intention, sometimes it needs a neutral person who is trustworthy and an expert on mental health issues of kids and adolescents whom the child needs to talk to.

Taking the Bull by the Horn

Given how common bullying is among zeners, it is important to bust two popular myths about bullying. One, only those who are bullied need help. And the second emanates from the first belief—that bullies are evil kids who must be tackled with an iron fist.

What is most important to remember here is that both bullies and those who are bullied are victims in this case. A National Institute of Child Health and Human Development (NICHD) research shows that anyone involved in bullying—those who bully others, those who are bullied, and those who bully and are bullied—are at increased risk of depression. Cyberbullying or those who are bullied electronically are also at a high risk of depression.

Most of the times, it is found that bullies come from families with parental disharmony or dysfunctionality. They need to be sensitized on how tormenting it could be for those whom they are bullying and what can be the consequences of the same. Bullying generally starts as a fun thing. Sometimes it is about avenging things that happen in the class; other times it is to assert superiority. In either case, the results can be disastrous, which is seldom understood or predicted by the bullies. That is why education and awareness are important. I am sure that those who bullied Mridul (Chapter 6) must not have thought that the outcome would be so dangerous and they too would get into serious trouble. There are schools who run anti-bullying workshops, show documentary films on bullying and its after effects, and train teachers to deal with bullies in the class as an ongoing activity. Having confidential reporting mechanism regarding cases of bullying is also important. Had there been anonymity in terms of reporting such incidents, then maybe some classmate of Mridul would have reported the issue and the matter could have been sorted before it reached a state of no return for Mridul. Additionally, schools need to actively engage school counsellors and train their teachers on how to notice such cases and deal with such issues.

Teen Suicides

Unfortunately, no one could save Mridul from taking his own life. Left behind were his broken parents, dazed friends and many unanswered questions. Mridul or Srishti (Chapter 5), who killed herself unable to handle her relationship, or zener teens killing themselves for grades prove that suicides do not have one common cause. They could have multiple causes. Whatever said and done, the problem is extremely serious. Kids and adolescents with suicidal tendencies generally suffer from severe low self-esteem, and the roots of their woes mostly lead up to dysfunctional families—broken families, conflictual families, families having extramarital affairs, 'parents not spending enough time with kids' families, career pressure families and highly result-oriented families. Ms Subhadra Gupta opines that there is always a correlation between the family environment and suicides. Generally, these kids are very

	Short Term Effects	Long Term Effects
B ull ie d	• Social Isolation • Low self esteem • Psychosomatic sym. • Sleep disturbance • Signs of anxiety and depression • Avoiding school	• Chronic Depression • Suicidal tendencies • PTSD • Anxiety disorder • Poor health • Substance abuse • Low levels of trust
B ull y	• Poor academic performance • High risk of truancy • Poor social relationships • High risk of substance abuse	• Antisocial behaviour • Risk of Spousal or child abuse • Substance abuse • Low probability of being educated and employed.

lonely and have no one to go to for comfort or for simply venting out freely, openly and without fear what they are going through in their lives.

According to the data published by the WHO, nearly 800,000 people die due to suicide every year, which is one person every 40 seconds. Suicide is the second leading cause of death among fifteen to twenty-nine-year-olds globally.

In India, one student kills himself/herself every hour.

Between 2014 and 2016, 26,476 students killed themselves in India.

Dr Roopesh says that although rising suicides are a sad reality among today's adolescents, suicides are rarely committed for frivolous reasons. If a teen takes his own life for not being given a smartphone or a bike, the real reason may be deeper. The boy might not have learnt self-regulation and hence any delayed gratification is not acceptable to him. The child may already be sad and the refusal may be the last straw. Instead of plainly saying no, a better reasoning and consistent reinforcement of the reality are necessary. A teen who kills himself for marks may have never been told that failure is also one option and one can always learn from it and move on. A hypercompetitive society and back-breaking pressure to perform can wreak havoc on a young mind. Many adolescents are not able to vent their feelings to anyone, and the stress bottles up and pushes them into isolation and depression.

States	Student Suicides in 2016	Student Suicides in 2014–2016 (Combined)
Maharashtra	1,350	3,771
West Bengal	1,147	2,532
Tamil Nadu	981	2,789
Madhya Pradesh	838	2,108

(continued)

(continued)

States	Student Suicides in 2016	Student Suicides in 2014–2016 (Combined)
Chhattisgarh	633	1,779
All Other States	4,525	13,497
India Total	9,474	26,476

Source: TOI. (2018, January 8). *One student kills self every hour in India. The Times of India.* Retrieved from https://timesofindia.indiatimes.com/india/one-student-kills-self-every-hour-in-india/articleshow/62407752.cms (accessed on 22 Nov 2019).

Warning Signs of Self-Harm

Suicides are very difficult to predict. Yet a vigilant parent and at times a vigilant teacher can do a lot more in terms of prevention, other than of course addressing the causal or triggering factors. The warning symptoms may be suspicious online activity, physical signs or changed social behaviour.

Suspicious Online Activity

- A child talking about self-injury or chatting online with those who have tried to inflict self-harm
- Becoming part of social media pages or online chat groups on self-harm
- Browsing websites on suicides

Physical Signs

- Suspicious looking scars or new ones over healed lesions, especially if lesions or cuts look more precise and not like an accident
- Wounds that do not heal and get worse
- Cuts on the same place repeatedly

Abnormal Social Behaviour

- Increased isolation and withdrawal symptoms
- Finding blades, penknives, first-aid kits, sterilizers or any such odd item with the child
- Avoiding social activities
- Wearing long-sleeves garments and trying to conceal forearms and wrists
- Refusing simple daily activities and play at school or at home
- Being nervous can be a sign of anxiety; uncontrolled anxiety can lead to suicide

There can be nothing more tragic and unfortunate than a young life snuffed out because of self-harm. The more I talked about preventing suicides and discussed with child and adolescent psychologists, the more it became clear to me that if a child has someone trustworthy to whom he/she can vent out everything without any fear, insecurity or concern, then most suicides are preventable. It just needs one such person to save a young life.

There are several suicide helplines run by various NGOs in India, but few are of real help. A report published by the *Times of India* in June 2018 reported that out of 22 suicide helpline numbers that it tried to reach, only 5 took the call, which included Vandrevala Foundation, SUMAITRI, COOJ, Lifeline Foundation and Saath.

Again, parents can play a significant role in this space. If they can create a safe environment, filled with trust and love, where there is openness, two-way uninterrupted communication, respect and tolerance for mistakes and failures, then the high suicide figures among teens in India can come down drastically. It is time to ask ourselves: Are we that one connect for our child to whom she/he can confide everything and not worry about consequences of telling everything to us? Are we?

The Parental Connection

Parents play a pivotal role in preventing and addressing mental health issues of kids and adolescents. They not only have the maximum window of influence over children but also have a sentimental attachment with them as well as a power to influence them like no one possibly can. Parental connection is not only the first connect for any child but also the most important connect. If this connection remains intact and thriving, then a lot of these issues can really be avoided or nipped in the bud before they can spring up an ugly face. As I wrote earlier, it is time to examine the entire gamut of parenting and understand the changing needs of today's kids and adolescents. Let us see what we can do as parents.

Open Communication

 I was driving through heavy traffic one morning. Bengaluru traffic can often get on to your nerves owing to the chaos and confusion especially during rush hours. Morning traffic is not the easiest to navigate. While I was stuck in the midst of one such commotion today morning, I noticed a school bus parallel to my car. Looking up I saw a bunch of toddlers sitting in the bus, happily talking. The bus was filled with lots of smiles, squeals of laughter and conversation. Just then I had eye contact with one of the toddler boys in the bus. While I did not know what to do at that moment, the boy waved at me with a big smile. I smiled back and waved at him. The experience further reinforced

that kids are not only better at communicating than us, but they also have an insatiable need to communicate, even with complete strangers at times.

Communication is the single most critical factor when it comes to preventing and addressing mental health issues of zeners. These children need to be heard; they need to vent out their anxieties, concerns and fears. It could be as simple as listening to their simple day stories or events/incidents at school. Asking them how their day was, if they had anything striking in the school that day and the like always helps them to open up and talk. Open communication is a must and needs time and attention more than anything else from the parents.

Logical Persuasion, Variable Restrictions

Consultant psychologist Atashi Gupta adds,

This is an intellectually much more mature generation than we think. As per my experience, the earlier age bands for various kinds of therapy are shifting. Earlier, for age groups of three–eleven, we mostly used to use play therapy since communication used to be an issue for very young kids. Play therapy is a psychotherapeutic approach that helps kids to explore their lives and freely express repressed thoughts and emotions through play. As children's experiences and knowledge are often communicated through play, it becomes an important vehicle for them to know and accept themselves and others. However, with today's kids I find that counselling works for much younger kids. I have counselled seven-year-olds, even a five-year-old child. Before counselling, we check the maturity, ability to adapt and ego strength of the child. My experience shows that these aspects are now exhibited by much younger kids. This is also a guide for the parents that nothing more than logical persuasion and rational conversations will work better in managing their kid's and adolescent's behaviour these days.

Considering Atashi's experience and observations as a consultant psychologist, we now know why Riya's (Chapter 5) parents were finding it difficult to dissuade her from going to the late night Christmas party. Another important observation here is that parents need to apply restrictions variably. Too many restrictions will not work for this generation. Simply putting one's foot down and using parental veto will not work.

And one more thing, do not mistake them for their young age. If a consultant psychologist finds a five-year-old ready for counselling, then we, parents, teachers or in whatever role we might be trying to engage with 'zeners', must not underestimate them for their age.

Clock Is Ticking

The most precious thing that parents can give to their children is their time. Zeners unfortunately are a generation of kids who are deprived of this very thing most of the times. I wrote this before and would like to emphasize the point one more time—only spending quality time with kids is not enough; quantum of time spent with kids is also important. Having at least one meal of the day together, going for a walk together, sometimes playing just for the heck of it, an occasional day out with kids and a small vacation—all of them help.

I see a tendency of parents to overcompensate on weekends as they are too busy on weekdays. This is just like eating whole week's food on one day. It leads to indigestion and flatulence. Weekend overcompensations also have the same effect and simply do not work. Parents often end up bribing the child and pampering him/her too much, which work the opposite way. Parents would have to find some time for kids on weekdays too. I know of a doctor couple who have managed their clinic and consultation timings in a manner that at least one of them is at home every evening with the kids. That has meant letting go of some consultation opportunities and making a little less money than they would have made otherwise. But the doctor couple tells me that they do not mind. They have earned enough to meet their needs, and they have the satisfaction that they are spending enough time with their children—a time that will never come back once they are grown up. They would not trade this for money.

Setting Appropriate Expectations

One of the things that I have never told my son is how much marks he should score in exams. I have clearly told him that for me his commitment matters, his understanding and learning matter, marks don't. Marks are essentially a by-product of all these and not necessarily the target that he should be working for. I know few more parents who do that, but unfortunately most parents put marks, percentage and grades as the primary goals for their children. Unreasonable performance expectations from parents can mount huge pressure on children, something that they often find unbearable and they develop a fear of failure, for failing would mean not meeting parental expectations and disappointing them, something that they feel guilty of doing. I know for sure that if my son resorts to rote learning and scores in excess of 90 per cent, he might still fail in the future, whereas, if he understands and learns the application of what he learns, he will have a far greater chance to succeed in the future. Parents do not necessarily stop at academic expectations from their children; they rather extend their expectations to sports, talent exams, extra-curricular activities and even to hobbies.

Failure Is an Option

The most creative are the ones who fail. Failure helps one to discover their greatness and innate abilities. When Thomas Edison, the inventor of the first electric bulb, was asked by the press about

the 10,000 times he had failed before finally inventing the electric bulb, he famously replied that he knew 10,000 ways of not making an electric bulb. A famous automobile company celebrates failure by giving out an award for the most creative failure of the month. The winner of the award is an employee or a group of employees who had the most stupendous learning from a failure that they experienced while working on a project. Failure is an option if we know how to learn from it. Why can't we teach the same thing to our kids? This will not only make them free of stress but also motivate them to try new things, experiment and be more creative in their approach.

Cultivate Interests

Having made our share of mistakes and we still do, there are few things we got right as parents. One of them being helping Arnab to develop a reading habit. However, we did not want to buy a book, give it to him and ask him to read. Instead, we decided to buy books and do something that makes him pick that book on his own and start reading it. So right from the time when he was very young, we would buy story books for him as per his age and instead of keeping books in the book rack, we ensured that books were visible and within his reach. The latter approach might make the house look a little less organized but then it is better to have books that are read than to have a 'library' where no one reads. We used to keep some of the books near his bedside. And the inevitable started to happen. Being sent to bed a little earlier than his usual time, he looked for an option to avoid sleep for some time. And books were the lowest hanging fruit for him. Arnab started reading. We ensured that before he finished one, we bought one more book for him. He always had something new to read. But not for once we asked him to read. Today nearing his teen, he is a voracious reader and often surprises me with his general awareness. There are occasions when he knows stuff that I do not have a clue about. Cultivating interest among children goes a long way in keeping them mentally occupied with productive and creative pursuits that give them happiness and satisfaction. However, it must be done in a way which ensures that these interests are developed organically in the children with no compulsion or force.

Socially Adept

Zeners are often poor in their social skills owing to too much of virtual socialization and hence need to be taught social skills at home. Those who have poor social skills are often at a greater risk of mental and physical health problems. People with poor social skills experience more loneliness and stress. This can negatively impact their health. A study headed by Chris Segrin of the University of Arizona for the first time found a relationship between poor social skills and poor mental and physical health. Parents can easily notice their child's struggle in a social situation and their inability to communicate properly, adapt to or be themselves in social situations. Also, kids with non-verbal learning disorder (NVLD), ADHD and social communication disorder (SCD) might have a problem with their social skills. Parents can do a lot to help or seek the help of an expert to help their children be adept at social skills.

Give Yourself a 'Like'

It is important for parents to teach children to like and love themselves. This should not be confused with inducing narcissism. Liking oneself means self-acceptance or in other words accepting the way we are. This helps reduce dissonance and trying to be someone else. Developing one's own personality, rather than living one's whole life trying to be someone else, is an important lesson. In this age of social media and public nature of life, comparison can often lead to a feeling of inequity. During such times, a strong sense of self-acceptance can be a big help. Liking oneself also means recognizing the qualities in oneself.

Children who learn to recognize their attributes also learn to further work on developing them and leverage them for better results and happiness. Liking oneself also means a bit of compassion for self. This can help reduce stress and avoid procrastination, according to Lindsay Holmes in the *Huffington Post*. Life has its own share of crests and troughs. When the chips are down, those who know to like themselves, are in touch with their inner self, can recognize their innate strengths and are more compassionate towards themselves are likely to be less prone to mental health issues and bounce back from adversity faster.

A study by David A. Sbarra, Hillary L. Smith and Matthias R. Mehl of the University of Arizona, published in a SAGE journal *Psychological Science*, revealed that 'the divorced individuals who spoke compassionately toward themselves were more able to bounce back in the months following the separation than those who spoke with self-criticism.'

Role Model

There is not a better role model for a child than the parent. Leading by example is the only way a child truly starts respecting his/her parents and starts imitating them as well. As discussed even in the previous chapter, asking a child to do what we ourselves cannot do as adults will cut little ice. If parents quarrel often and argue loudly in front of the child, then it is bound to affect him both in his behaviour and psychologically. In scenarios where a child finds his/her father or mother as a role model, they not only have better mental health but can also trust their parents more in difficult situations. They would also communicate more and listen more.

A letter written by a 12-year-old girl (Pratiksha) about her father.

MY FATHER & HIS LIFE

MY Father and his life story is amazing to hear. You want to hear? He has been an amazing dad from the time I was born and even after my brother. He worked in several companies and at last left all of them and started his own company. He got fed up hearing, seeing... complaining about the potholes in India so he started a company named potholeraja. He teaches in schools about life. He loves sports from the time he joined NCC. He now runs & does shading too. He got the best credit award also in NCC. He read many plains too. He likes drawing. has got inspired by his father's inspir me too. He also knew bhathanatyam from his early childhood. He recently went fortrekking in buronghati from India hikes. Do you want to know what his NAME is?

PRATAP B

Concern Not Criticism

Overcriticism is detrimental to the mental health of children. A study by a team of researchers led by Kiera James from the University of Birmingham, published in the *Journal of Clinical Child & Adolescent Psychology*, has found that children with critical parents avoid paying attention to the faces expressing any type of emotion. This avoidance is like a coping mechanism they develop to avoid the negative expression on the face of their parents when they are criticizing. But this behaviour also makes them avoid positive expression on faces of others communicating with them. This therefore might affect their relationship with others and could be one of the reasons why children who are exposed to high levels of criticism may be at a greater risk of depression and anxiety.

Parents are an important source of feedback and one of the earliest relationships of children through which children make a sense of themselves and develop self-worth and self-esteem. These feedbacks also make them feel themselves as capable, competent and loved. The two main types of feedback given by a parent include praise and criticism. There are now strong researches to indicate that praise or positive statements used by parents, which are often accompanied by parental warmth, responsiveness and warmth, can boost the competence and confidence of a child, whereas criticism or negative statements expressed by parents to convey their disapproval may instead be counterproductive, contrary to the expectations of the parents. This might make the child more aggressive, defiant and have other behavioural problems. Harsh criticism may not only kill intrinsic motivation but also breed a feeling of shame in them. Often, labels are given to children by parents or elders in this state of angry criticism that are often demeaning and condescending.

Positive parenting requires us to be able to often use praise but avoid overpraising or false-praising at the same time. Anything that we wish to correct in our child needs a proper response. We as parents often 'react' to our child's action or behaviour; we seldom 'respond'. The response or the attempt to correct them must not only be thought from a short-term perspective; long-term impacts of our disciplining and the life lesson that we are going to teach them also hold importance. Hence, any corrective statement must be expressed as a concern or why a parent feels genuinely concerned about a particular action or behaviour of a child. It should be explained to them why they need to correct themselves and how it is going to otherwise affect them in the short and long terms.

No Comparisons

Recognizing that every child is unique and has his/her own sets of strengths, orientation and creative inclination is fundamental to parenting. Any comparison either with another sibling or with a friend or any other child is always going to impact them negatively. Comparison often makes them feel belittled, less loved, less wanted, less competent and less confident and at the same time puts undue pressure on them in trying to be someone else. Comparison done by parents can also instil in them a sense of hypercompetitiveness that again might magnify as they grow up as adults and cause various mental and physical health-related problems.

Non-violence

Any sort of violence with a child or in front of a child at home is going to adversely impact his/her mental health. There is no difference of opinion about it. Dr Roopesh strongly warns against hitting or spanking the child. We have already discussed how it negatively impacts their mental health. Parents physically abusing each other in front of the child or at home where the child eventually comes to know can scar him/her psychologically forever.

Stop Nagging

'Cross the road safely', 'Keep your phone safely', 'Do not go to any other child's apartment', 'Do not board the lift alone', 'Do not stay out after dark'—these are a set of instructions that are repeated to Samuel by his mother whenever he goes out to play in his building community play area. He has got so used to it that he hardly listens when every evening his mother repeats these dictums. He just does not bother.

Yes, it is true that children 'tune out' their nagging parents. Melanie Greenberg, psychologist and parenting expert, states,

When parents go on and on, kids tune them out. Researchers have shown that the human brain can keep only four 'chunks' of information or unique ideas in short-term (active) memory at once. This amounts to about 30 seconds or one or two sentences of speaking.

Many zeners who I interviewed for my book told me in common about nagging as an irritating behaviour in their parents, which they would like to change in them.

Nagging creates resentment and makes a child feel over-controlled and less competent, and researchers say that nagging makes teens feel 'manipulated'. They are at a stage where they want more freedom, and nagging only appears as a ploy of parents to chain them and control them in all their actions. That creates resentment and defiance. Research also clearly shows how nagging can spoil the relationship and connect between a child and a parent.

Parents have their own reasons when it comes to nagging. Many mothers have told me, 'What else I would do? Even after telling him so many times, my child does not follow the instructions properly.' Parents nag to allay their fears about the safety of their child, in their anxiety to make their child perfect or as an authority figure to control their action and behaviour to teach them the right lessons for life. While the desired outcome may not be bad at all, the approach of nagging is definitely a wrong chosen path. Instead, making the child take responsibility of his/her own actions is important. Mrs Singh tells me about her twelve-year-old son Sunny,

Instead of asking my child every evening to sit for completing his school work, I asked him to make his own study plan and timetable for home. Once he made it, I just asked him to follow what he has himself made. That made a big difference, although it took time. But eventually I did not have to ask him to sit for his homework every day. He started following his own plan and timetable.

Isn't that what we are trying to achieve as parents? Mrs Singh's approach not only made her stop nagging but also made Sunny learn the value of responsibility and accountability early in his life.

Understand Developing Needs

When you hug a child, never let him/her go before he/she releases the embrace, for you never know how much love a child needs. Understanding the developing needs of a child is extremely important. Small kids might need more physical affection, while as kids grow up, and remember zeners grow up faster than kids of the previous generation, they might have more emotional and intellectual needs. A mother talking about her eight-year-old zener was telling me how everyday she would hug and kiss her son while bidding him goodbye just before he boarded the school bus. While this ritual was acceptable to him till a few months back, now he finds it embarrassing. One day he told his mother after coming back from school not to hug or kiss him in front of his school bus friends. Needs can change and responding to them is what parents can best do. However, it is important to remember not to pre-empt anything and there is no standard rule. Observation and remaining in touch with the child are the keys to understanding their needs.

Validate Feelings

Parents should never dismiss the feelings of their child. When Vineetha found her ten-year-old son romantically inclined towards one of his classmates and a bit heartbroken that the girl had brushed off his advances, she initially found it funny

that her son could nurture such feelings at a young age, but then she decided to acknowledge his feelings and talk to him openly about the same. Zeners do up-age, and hence such feelings for the opposite gender are not very uncommon yet it is important to remember that it is nothing compared to what a young adult man would feel for a damsel. It is more like an innocent love. But even at that age, zeners can feel snubbed and dejected at being rejected by the one they have been attracted to. The approach helped and soon her son had learnt to cope with the snubbing and also realized that he needs to grow up a little more to think about such affairs and handle them maturely. Dr Roopesh emphasizes, 'Respecting and acknowledging the feelings of the child are very important. Parents must acknowledge their child's feelings and just not brush those off or dismiss those. Have a positive regard for your child and learn to respect their emotions and thoughts.' It definitely contributes to their positive mental health, as it makes them feel secure about their feelings and know that they can trust their parents to share anything without fearing being belittled, embarrassed or being brushed aside.

Time Travel

Parents must teach their child to look at a long-term view of success. Like they may not necessarily be the first ranker in the class or be the head boy or head girl but they can still have equally successful educational pursuit and/or careers in the long term. Zeners also look for instant gratification and want the success quick and fast. If it, however, does not come at that pace, they are also dejected soon and can harbour negative cognitive beliefs. Helping them recognize the fallacy of comparisons, the fact that long-term view of success is more important than just depending on short-term success and that they themselves are their best competition is the key. This is, however, possible only when parents themselves recognize the same for themselves, their lives and their view of the life.

No Castles in the Air

Learning to deal with failures and disappointments is important right from a young age. Parents should never give false hopes to their child, as that would further worsen the matter as and when the child finds those hopes dashed as well. There is a thin line between not letting your child feel a sense of hopelessness and in giving false hopes to him. For instance, when he loses, instead of telling him that 'Next time you will definitely win', it is better to tell them that 'I am sure that you will learn from your mistakes this time around and next time you will prepare even better and perform better than this time'. The second one is more realistic and has higher probability of occurrence. Besides, even if the next time the child does not end as the winner, he would still have the satisfaction of performing better. With the latter approach, the child eventually has a chance of continuously improving his own performance, rather than competing with others.

Spotting Grey

Life is not always black or white; there are abundant shades of grey. It is not always either 'yes' or 'no'; there are many instances of yes and no, both being conditional. There is not just always pure right or wrong; right or wrong can also be relative and perceptual. A child generally looks at things expecting homogeneity. Parents play an important role in helping the child recognize the heterogeneous nature of the world and spot the shades of grey. This can play a very important role in how a child learns to regulate emotions and feelings. Further, the child also learns how others view them or perceive their words and/or actions and are affected by them.

Rock Solid

A child must have confidence that, 'No matter what, I will always find my parents standing behind me, always. They might scold me when I am wrong, correct me and at times get angry with me as well, but they will always be with me.' This confidence is critical to not allow a child to get into a state of despair and hopelessness. This rock solid confidence in a child about their parents can not only make them more open in terms of communication but also prevent anxiety, depression and suicides.

David Marquet says,

Parenting is like leadership in that you are trying to gradually move your children from dependence to independence. This is done by continuously assessing their maturity and competence and inviting them to take greater and greater control of their decisions. Ideally, by the time they leave the house, they've learned to make wise decisions and can safely and effectively enter the world.

Undoubtedly, parents play the most crucial and pivotal role, especially in preventing and/or identifying the mental health issues of a child.

Role of Schools and Teachers

The role of schools and teachers in supporting positive mental health of kids and adolescents must also not be misjudged at the same time. After parents, teachers are the next most important authority figure managing them, and after home, school is the next best place for socialization as well as the only place that engages in formal communication and reinforcements. Teachers may at times be the first to identify a mental health issue in a child which parents may overlook due to limited data points.

Holistic Whole

Schools can create a positive environment and a tenet that build on the holistic strength of a child instead of focusing on only academic performance. This reduces overreliance on marks as a benchmark of a student's success and ignores other variables that may have equally big impact on the overall development of a child's talents and personality. Dr Sarah Buckley, Professor Fiona McNicholas and Dr Blánaid Gavin, consultant psychiatrists at St Patrick's University Hospital, Dublin, and authors of the book *Mental Health in Children and Adolescents: A Guide for Teachers*, state,

The role that schools and teachers play in promoting positive mental health in children should not be underestimated. Creating a school ethos which promotes and builds strength among students, whatever their academic profile, can turn risk into resilience and significantly reduce the prevalence and impact of mental health disorders.

Any sort of comparison or overcriticism that the child is subjected to in school can create negative stress in him and often make him susceptible to being shamed or mocked by peers. Instead, if the uniqueness of every child is identified and they are encouraged to leverage from the same, they are going to do much better both academically and in other intra- and extra-curricular activities.

Life Skills

Teaching life skills to the kids and adolescents goes a long way in helping them develop a right mindset and in prevention of mental health issues. Prathap Bhimsen Rao, who is faculty at EFIL Pvt. Ltd (Education for Integrating Life) and imparts life skill training to school students across the state of Karnataka in India, states,

The traditional approach teaches children 'I need to have what I don't have.' However, the life skill approach emphasizes on 'How do I use what I have?' It teaches them how to capitalize the situation to the best. For instance, some children may be made to believe that since they are not good at communication skill, they are social unfits. They do not get accepted in social groups. Such stigmas often are the cause of mental health problems.

Prathap further states,

When we find kids who are different from others, we tend to stereotype solutions. Such an approach boomerangs and is instead counterproductive to the wellness of the children. They may still be good at communication in more comfortable settings. Life skills focus on how a right context and relevance can be created for the kids. Our focus is how they capitalize the skill that they already possess and how they use that skill in an appropriate life context.

The most important starting point for life skills is what beliefs one has and what are the values drawing out of those beliefs. For example, one likes to share things. This belief is connected to a value system that he/she has developed by observing their parents or elder siblings. Sharing is a value and a belief is connected to that value. However, most of the times children are not clear as to what they believe or, as discussed before, they may harbour wrong cognitive beliefs. If they are not clear about their beliefs, they are also not clear about their values. And when they are not clear about their values, they do not value a thing, which also makes them feel devalued. This impacts their attitudes, personalities and behaviours. The fundamental starting point for life skills is to connect values and beliefs and, once that clarity is established, to identify how all these can be connected to life.

Prathap adds that till date EFIL has imparted life skills to more than 30,000 students over a period of 12 years. A longitudinal research study using a control group helped them establish three major impacts of life skills. The study was done over a period of eight years. A control group was also used, which comprised students who had not undergone life-skill training. The study revealed some major impacts among students who had undergone life-skill training.

One of the major objectives of life-skill training was to understand whether those who went through the training saw themselves as victims or masters of circumstances. It is not that those who had undergone life-skill training did not face any problems, adversities or issues in their lives, but whenever they came across difficult circumstances, they considered themselves the masters of those circumstances, rather than victims. They were able to draw the right beliefs from their value systems and to deal with those issues without succumbing to them and getting mentally depressed. Prathap who takes care of research, technology and teaching at EFIL states,

These days, a lot of kids as young as those in sixth or seventh standard mention about depression, fight with parents or siblings, or that they do not want to connect with the society. They bring a lot of judgemental aspects to their life, which affects them mentally as well as physically. Life skills teach them how not to think of them as victims and avoid being judgemental about circumstances or contexts and deal with them being on the top of the same, looking at themselves as being larger than the problem.

The other impacts were the ability to give back to the society and community, ability to learn continuously from experiences, an attitude of valuing both the ends and the means, and finally the ability to see things from a long-term perspective.

Positive Discipline

Connection before correction is the fundamental principle of positive discipline that is based in tenets of positive psychology. We have already seen the kind of negative impacts corporal punishments can have on the mental health of kids and adolescents. Positive discipline is based on maintaining dignity and respect through 'kindness' and 'firmness' at the same time.

The criteria for positive discipline are as follows:

- Does it help students feel a sense of connection?
- Is it effective in long term as well as in short term?
- Does it teach social competencies and life skills for good character?
- Is it respectful? (Kind and firm)
- Does it invite children to discover how capable they are and how to use their power constructively?

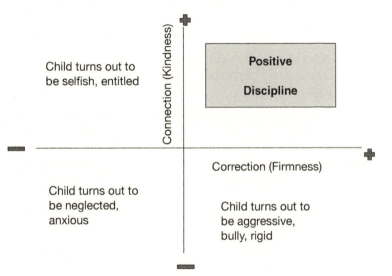

Positive discipline is based on Adlerian psychology, which includes the following:

- Children are social beings. Behaviour is goal-oriented. Primary goal is belonging and significance.
- A misbehaving child is a discouraged child.
- *Gemeinschaftsgefühl* or a feeling of 'community engagement' or 'social interest'—this Adlerian term is used to describe one's connectedness and interest in the well-being of others,

which enhances or preconditions psychological health. The revolutionary notion was proposed by Alfred Adler.
- Dignity and respect for all.
- Mistakes are wonderful opportunities to learn.
- Make sure that the message of love gets through.

Roadblocks

External Therapy is a luxury only afforded to some and counselling services in school are either limited or lacking. The number of trained psychologists working in the mental health sector is very low: only 0.047 per lakh. Expenditure on mental health occupies only 0.06 percentage of the government's health budget. And rather unsurprisingly, the participation of informal human resources (such as family and friend support groups) in India, according [to] the World Health Organization (WHO) is 'Not Routine'. (The Economist, 2019)

Health Professionals Working in India's Mental Health Sector
(Rate per 100,000)

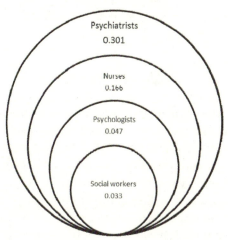

Source: https://www.who.int/mental_health/evidence/atlas/profiles/ind_mh_profile.pdf (accessed on 22 Nov 2019).

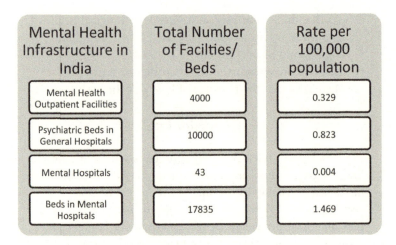

Mental Health Infrastructure in India	Total Number of Facilties/ Beds	Rate per 100,000 population
Mental Health Outpatient Facilities	4000	0.329
Psychiatric Beds in General Hospitals	10000	0.823
Mental Hospitals	43	0.004
Beds in Mental Hospitals	17835	1.469

Source: https://www.who.int/mental_health/evidence/atlas/profiles/ind_mh_profile.pdf (accessed on 22 Nov 2019).

The low number of mental health workers and poor mental health infrastructure are huge roadblocks in tackling mental health issues in India. Government hospitals like NIMHANS are overcrowded, and the demand far exceeds the supply. Private mental care cannot be afforded by the poor.

Way Forward

Undoubtedly, there is an urgent need to ramp up the mental health infrastructure and have more qualified mental health professionals. However, this also calls for both informal human resources especially the parents to realize that they need to play a bigger role in their children's lives. The Generation Z kids' susceptibility to mental health issues is well established now and parents can do a lot in being more vigilant, creating the right environment at home, providing psychological support to their children, remaining aware of the warning signs of setting in of a mental health issue and knowing when to seek professional help.

At the same time, there is also a need for teachers to hone their counselling skills. Most schools cannot afford a full-time counsellor. After parents, teachers are the next biggest window of reference as far as children are concerned. They can not only set the right context, implement positive discipline and impart life skills but also spot the warning signs of mental health issues among kids and adolescents much faster. A paper presented by Susanna Wai Ching Lai-Yeung in the 2013 International Congress on Clinical and Counselling Psychology, titled 'The Need for Guidance and Counselling Training for Teachers', argued,

> Teachers have multiple roles to perform nowadays. To fulfil their roles professionally, teachers need to be competent in their responsibilities towards their students inside and outside the classroom. One important teacher role inside and outside the classroom is to provide guidance and counselling to students…. Guidance work is preventive and developmental in nature whereas counselling is more of supportive, remedial work.

The relevance of discussions in this chapter, which primarily examined and emphasized the role of parents and teachers in preventing and addressing mental health issues of zeners, draws from such findings. Not to forget that even professional help is only possible if these two important authority figures are more cognizant of their roles in ensuring good mental health of their children.

References

Economist. (2019, March 14). Most mental-health problems are untreated. Trained laypeople can help. *The Economist*. Retrieved from https://www.economist.com/leaders/2019/03/14/most-mental-health-problems-are-untreated-trained-laypeople-can-help (accessed on 22 Nov 2019).

Lai-Yeung, S. W. (2014). The need for guidance and counselling training for teachers. *Procedia-Social and Behavioral Sciences, 113,* 36–43.

8

LEARNING TO LIVE WITH PARADOXES

━━━◆◆◆━━━

Teenpreneurs

Talrop Grolius is not just another company and there is also nothing ordinary about it. Would you believe it if I tell you that this company is not a creation of seasoned IT professionals or venture capitalist-backed entrepreneurs? Instead, this is a company started by 12 school kids in South Kalamassery near Cochin, a small sleepy town in the state of Kerala, India. Yes, you heard me right.

These dynamic dozen, some in their 10th grade and others in the 9th grade of their school, were mentored by a visionary person named Safeer. He learnt coding

THE DYNAMIC DOZEN

Haleela Fathima AS

Adhil Muhammad

Vaisakh Raj A

Mahadev Ratheesh

Saira S

Alamsha A S

Muhammed Siyad S

Fahad Salman F N

Meenakshi Saril

Yasir Muhammed

Rubi A S

Athulya S Nath

at a very young age and strongly believed that technology is the future. He had a brainwave and he wondered to himself, if adults can learn coding, why can't this be taught to kids? They stood a better chance of learning it in lesser time and mastering it, as their minds were less cluttered. Hence, they had to do considerably less unlearning. Safeer approached the principal of his alma mater, the school where he had studied in his childhood. The consent of the principal changed it all. This was the beginning of Talrop Grolius, which means 'grow like us'. A bunch of students were selected based on different aspects such as logical sense and typing speed and more so based on their passion. The dynamic dozen were trained in website and software development. They were also trained in client management, client relations, finance and other aspects of running a company. Today, Talrop Grolius is a technology company run by these young coders, and they provide IT services at very economical rates compared to other companies. In the near future, these kids will focus their energies on developing mobile applications besides services such as website designing, website development, server set-up and domain support services that they already offer.

Amazing, isn't it? Throughout this book, such exceptional zeners are featured, but do not be mistaken that it's only these handful few. This entire generation is special and extraordinary, the real power of which the world is still to witness in its entirety. They are the future and hope for this planet and for this universe. Born in an age of technology, information revolution and social media explosion, this generation is a powerhouse ready to explode.

Surojit Dhar, father of a five-year-old boy, says, 'I find all kids of this generation very forthcoming and confident. Recently, we had a children's day celebration at office and all the kids were so impressive. I do not remember to be anything like them when I was their age.' He continues,

These kids process information so fast that it leaves me feeling amazed. The other day I was watering the plants. I thought after watering the plants I will prepare breakfast for my five-year-old son Nihaan. Just then, he came to me and asked, 'What are you doing, Daddy?' I told him that I was watering the plants. To this, he immediately quipped, 'OK, you are giving breakfast to the plants.' I smiled and nodded in affirmation. Then he went to ask me if plants needed lunch and dinner as well. It might appear very silly for us adults but for a five-year-old boy to relate watering of plants with their equivalent of a breakfast and co-relate their other intakes as his equivalent of consuming lunch and dinner are really worthy of praise.

This is true and echoed by more parents. 'Zeners are knowledgeable'. Dr Shetty talks about his younger daughter Pranjala who is barely ten years old,

One day, Pranjala asked me if dogs could donate blood. I did not know this subject too well but half listening to her question, I told her that dogs cannot donate blood to each other as blood groups matching is difficult. But Pranjala actually knew the answer. She was just testing my knowledge. Immediately she quipped, 'No, dogs can donate blood to other dogs. For first-time donation, any dog can donate blood to any other dog. However, if further donations are done, then blood groups need to be matched.'

Being brought up in a volatile, uncertain, complex and ambiguous (VUCA) world and in an era of start-up culture, zeners have the mind of an entrepreneur. Subhashish, father to a seven-year-old boy, narrates an interesting incident,

My son Ayan goes to play with his apartment friends downstairs every evening. One such evening when he went down to play, I accompanied him. I observed that some kids were gathered in a circle. Upon closer observation, I found that one of them had learnt a technique to make paper earrings. While Ayan played, I saw how they made the earrings and later sold them to the elders who were around. That was amazingly entrepreneurial. I don't think as kids we would think that way. We would probably make the earrings but would hardly think about selling them for a price.

Subhashish is right. The amazement of most members of the older generation at such behaviour is their inability to appreciate that culturally too Generation Z is different from the previous generation as also from their own parents. This cultural difference reflects in various dimensions. Zeners are global citizens in the truest sense. Their life is influenced by not only their national and regional cultures but also by other cultures across the world. They have friends from different parts of the world. Most of them have travelled outside their country or have met people from different nationalities. In the era of ubiquitous media, they are aware of world affairs in their area of interest. They follow international icons and are influenced by them.

Generation Z Values

Source: Based on an extensive survey of over 1,000 participants from Gen Z, done over a period of more than one year.

Surojit opines,

This generation is a very egalitarian generation. As a keen observer of global politics as well as Indian politics, I can say that with a lot of conviction. In India, we have caste-based reservation. With this new generation, I see a difference in the way they perceive reservations. Political parties will find it difficult to buy their loyalty by doling out reservation. They are like, 'OK, you can give me reservation but that will not influence me or my decision to choose.' That is revolutionary, I believe.

He further comments,

This generation is very high on gender neutrality. We never were as much and found it difficult to break the gender stereotypes. I know a girl who plays tabla and a boy who loves playing the flute and they are determined to follow their passion, although the society may see these instruments to be not best matches as per gender perception, with tabla being stereotyped for male and flute being seen as subtler and therefore stereotyped feminine. This generation has lesser inhibitions and is breaking gender stereotypes, the reason I call them gender neutral.

The cultural difference of zeners does not come without its own share of criticism from the older generation. Sumana, like most mothers of zeners, is not convinced of her daughter's sense of safety and sense of being careful. She says,

It is very difficult to convince this generation why they should not do certain things, especially ones that danger their safety. For instance, if I tell my teenage daughter not to wear certain types of garments while going to some places, I am often misunderstood. She fails to understand that there are some people who may try to take advantage of her. This generation is difficult to control.

What will you call this—a cultural difference or a generational gap? Sumana is worried as a mother but her daughter sees no reason for her worry. Remember Amrutha? We read about her in the first chapter. When I spoke to her parents, I found that it was more a cultural gap. Dr Jeethendra Shetty and his wife Vidya do not like their daughter wearing shorts. Although there is no pressure on Amrutha on this matter, they have conveyed to her very clearly that they do not like her wearing shorts. And while she listens to them when it comes to wearing attire outside home, when it comes to being at house, she wears shorts. A matter of comfort and style for the daughter is an issue of culture, family prestige and customs for her parents. Zeners display conditional followership. They will not accept anything without questioning and only if they are convinced would they follow the same, whether it is a tradition or a ritual or a practice/rules or people. The followership is conditional. Dr Jeethendra Shetty opines,

Zeners treat themselves as equals. It is not easy to bog them down. As kids, we did not have the permission to talk when adults were talking or answer them back, even if they were wrong. Few kids were playing in our gated community complex. Few adults who were taking an evening walk objected to them playing on the grass. These kids in turn told the adults that if they wanted to join them they were welcome, else they should mind their own business.

Sumana says,

My daughter will always ask me about any rule that she has to follow at home, especially with respect to religious rituals. Once she asked me why vegetarian food cannot be kept along with non-vegetarian food, as is the custom in most Hindu families who worship the deity at home. When we were kids, we just used to follow what our parents used to ask us to do, but not this generation. For everything, they have a 'why'.

Sumana corroborates the conditional followership aspect of zeners. They are assertive and exposed to world media and cultures. They are aware and armed with information. Naturally, they have developed a need to know what they are following and without being convinced of the rationale, they refuse to accept the same.

There is no denying the fact that this is an extraordinary generation but at the same time it is also true that they too have a paradoxical life much like the millennials, though their paradoxes are different and more in number compared to the millennial generation.

A Dozen Paradoxes

On the one hand, digital technologies, gadgets and platform offer a world of opportunities to zeners, while on the other, they pose serious health hazards, loneliness, depression and susceptibility to online bullying if used for a long time and in an unrestricted manner (digital paradox). They have been exposed to global ubiquitous media, World Wide Web and social media from an early age, which has made them aware and empowered, but this digital unsupervised exposure often exposes them to uncouth and undesirable material, which in the absence of guidance gets misinterpreted and misconstrued (exposure paradox). Today, they have access to an ocean of information at the touch of a button. In fact, they have so much information that they do not need to go to school for gaining knowledge. Yet sifting through the vast mass of information to know what, why, where, how and when to use the information is really a challenge (information paradox). They have evolved learning approaches and styles and can use sophisticated technology-enabled learning tools, yet they find themselves in an education system that is yet to evolve as much as the learners have in terms of educating for a job or a career (learning paradox). Zeners are born to plenteousness much facilitated by their parents' zeal to provide them everything that they could not enjoy as children, yet they see temporariness as the new world order. They are, like their parents, not sure if everything is going to be there the next day or next moment (plenteousness paradox). They find themselves spoilt for choice when it comes to goods, services or brands, yet they are not completely unaware of how rising inflation is burning holes in the pockets of their parents, often dragging them into the EMI whirlpool (choice paradox). The provisions mean that their parents have to work hard and work late hours and often over weekends. This on the one hand makes them more independent and adaptable but on the other leaves them lonelier as they get to spend much less time with their parents compared to the previous generations. While their parents provide them with the best of gadgets to keep them occupied, to afford these luxuries, they are working long hours which keeps them away from their children. Parents don't have the time to answer the zillion questions zeners have that emanate from their exposure to technology and information. I like to call it the home alone paradox. Much like the home alone child, they become independent and adaptable but missing parents makes them lonelier and stranded with questions and no answers (home alone paradox). They have parents who worry a lot about their career while they are still in schools, which probably means that their parents are better prepared monetarily and informatively to combat the career challenges that their kids would face in the future; but this also means heightened career obsession of parents about their kid's career leading to too many and too much expectations, often at the cost of their child's passion (career paradox). They are a generation that is creative, entrepreneurial and not risk-averse, yet the pressure to perform and to succeed is often too much (performance paradox). They live in a connected world, a world where network maps are significant. Yet this network is mostly virtual, leaving them with fewer real experiences. They have started assuming that virtual is real in itself. Their real-life relationships take time to develop and often they find easier to communicate through WhatsApp and Instagram than having a face-to-face conversation. Their lack of touch with the real often leads to convulsions in their relationships (virtual paradox). Zeners are culturally more diverse, inclusive and open, having been exposed to the global culture, yet they often find that hijacked by rising religious, regional and ethnic fundamentalism. Globalization has lowered national boundaries when it comes to business, but on the other hand the growing hatred and violence in the name of religion has held humanity for a ransom (globalization paradox). The high potential, high intelligence and high ability of this generation are true on the one hand, but in the world that they live in, they find their homes changing, pressures mounting and the world becoming more predatory; they find themselves prey to anxiety and depression and vulnerable to poor mental health. Their susceptibility is often disproved by many terming it as jitters of growing up, but such people fail to count the transformed environment that actually magnifies their challenges (devil's paradox). I call the last one devil's paradox because the devil's proof is the rational predicament that while evidence proves the existence of something, the lack of evidence fails to disprove it. In effect, the opposing statement's lack of proof makes the statement true in some sense.

The bad news is that Gen Z are inflicted with these paradoxes when they are still kids and adolescents, but believe me the good news is also the same. Unlike millennials, where by the time we realized, the damage had already been done, in the case of zeners or Gen Z, we still have time to get our act together as they are in their formative years.

The Fireside Chat

Writing this book has been a wonderful and exhilarating journey. I had an opportunity to talk to countless people and listen to their interesting experiences, not only from India but also from other parts of the world. Interestingly, my better half was with me in almost all the interviews and discussions that I conducted. And befittingly so, since leaving her out would mean cutting down on 50 per cent of my experience as a parent of a boy who is now in his teens, all the more so because the buck really stops on parents. They were, are and will be the most significant influence on their children.

It was a Sunday afternoon and we were having our usual weekend conversation. But that day, the discussion veered around the book and we started talking about the various people we met—the kids, so many parents, teachers, psychologists, doctors and others. Vandana joked how I used to virtually chase people with my sound recorder to get them talking. We had a hearty laugh together. But on a serious note, it has been the most enriching and learning experience for both of us. We learnt what to learn, what to unlearn and what not to learn, all at the same time. That evening, Vandana and I had one of our most intellectually stimulating discussions. There could not have been a better way to finish this book than to share our discussion with all of you.

Show Me the Way

Zeners are a generation who will not accept anything that they do not find the adults following themselves. They are stubborn; they question and argue. I was surprised and pleasantly so to find that Arnab has finished writing his first novel while I was writing this book. I am yet to read his book, but I never implied implicitly or explicitly or expect that he would like writing just because he is my son. But he seems to be taking to writing as fish takes to water. It is very simple; if we want our kids to do something, develop good habits and display good behaviour, then first, we as parents have to do and believe in that. Parents who are addicted to their phones asking their kids to show restraint is a futile attempt.

No Substitute of Time

I remember, as a child, my brother and I used to wait for our father to come back from office to pull him into a game of cricket, badminton or table tennis. And he would happily join us. At times, we would not even let him have his cup of evening tea, but he never complained. As we grew up, we found him approachable and more like a friend. The time that parents spend with their kids cannot be substituted with anything else, especially not with material comforts, toys or gadgets. Agnibesh believes that zeners are a much more adaptable generation. He opines, 'We both are working professionals and have to plan our time with our son. But despite being very young, I think he understands that my parents are working hard and they do not have much time. He is so very adaptable.' But having known both Agnibesh and his wife Rupasa,

I have seen them making efforts and taking turns to spend time with their only son, despite having a full-time caretaker at home. Spending quality time is important, but the quantum of time spent with kids is equally important. When a child thinks that his smartphone is his best friend, it essentially signifies failure of us as parents. The emotional vulnerability of zeners, their susceptibility to factors outside the house and their poor state of mental health in general can be avoided to a large extent if parents spend time with their children.

Communicate and Build Trust

Spending time also helps in developing communication between parents and their children. Often, the subtle nuances are missed in communication with the child when the connection is poor. A mother once told me how often her second child used to tell her that she did not trust him. Her son always felt that she trusted the elder sibling, his sister. She tried her best to explain how she trusted him as well. But this did not quite convince him. One night, when the entire family returned from an outing, this lady gave keys to her son and asked him to open the door. This is when her son quipped, 'OK, now you trust me.' The lady was surprised, but she learnt a very important lesson of her life. She must have thought about a million things to tell her son to make him believe that she trusted him, yet it took such a small action to build the trust really. Building confidence in the child that 'if you make a mistake, I will correct you but no matter what I will stand by you' goes a long way in avoiding alienation of the child in his growing-up years.

Empathy Is Critical for Connection

Understanding the zeners and developing and exhibiting empathy are critical for establishing a connection with them. Viola Isaac is one such example we remember, one of the best teachers we ever met. She was the principal of my son's school for a year, and she played a very important role in the life of my son in his early schooling years. Her abilities to empathize with the kids of all ages and connect with them was amazing and it commanded both respect and love from them. We as parents need to have a similar kind of empathy, which does not border on the lines of sympathy and mollycoddling but at the same time makes the child feel that he/she is understood, heard and not abandoned emotionally.

Real Has More Dimensions

Zeners are losing touch with the real world and real relationships. Born in the era of social media and virtual networking, somewhere the real relationships have taken a back seat. Few months back, when we had nine of our close relatives visiting us, we had to make some makeshift arrangements in our two-bedroom apartment, as everyone could not have a room for themselves. For the first time, my son did not have his own room and his own bed to sleep. I saw his concealed irritation during the first two days. It was his first such experience in his 13 years on this planet. But as time progressed, I saw how he mingled with everyone and gradually forgot about his discomfort. Such experiences are good for him. He learns the value of real relationships, emotional bonding and sharing his space with others. After all, life is more than just Instagram!

Steer Clear of Fear

Fear-based management is really not the best way to manage this generation. They will simply disconnect and disengage. Fear often leads to concealing and depression. Disciplining is the single most bone of contention between parents. Often, parents disagree between themselves as to how to discipline the child. The stricter parent accuses the lenient parent of spoiling the child, while the latter accuses the former of being the terror in the house. It is a delicate balance between being strict and lenient. Research shows that the good cop–bad cop parenting is more beneficial for kids. A new research published in the *Journal of Child Psychology and Psychiatry* shows that parents need to assume good cop and bad cop roles as per situation and at times the roles can be switched between parents. Researcher Dr Judith Locke believes, 'Parents need to be confident in themselves in positive, warm parenting. Parents should meet in the middle and offer consistency. It is never going to be good for kids if both parents are too tough. Screaming and hitting won't ever work.'

Covert Operations Are Blinded by Light

Openness in the relationship between zeners and their parents assumes greater significance in an age where technology has made everything available to everyone. Children are exposed to a lot of sexually explicit and violent material online. No amount of privacy setting and child locks can prevent that. Parents hence need to keep it open and relaxed at home. There may be some awkward moments, but then a confident, frank parent can navigate through these situations far better than one who creates a culture of taboo at home. Porn addiction, teenage pregnancy and sex-related crimes among teens and pre-teens, all are to a large extent creation of this taboo culture at home. A right way of knowing things and satisfying one's curiosity is better and healthier than the 'covert operations' that always complicate the things.

Kids Are Not Superheroes

I know how much we love superheroes, but let's not start bringing them out of the screen and start viewing them in our kids. This is absurd and unrealistic. How many of us adults can do everything?

None, right? Then why do we expect our kids to learn music, score 99 per cent in exams, be good in sports, represent talent shows or events, learn robotics, win competitions, all at the same time, whether they like it or not? This epidemic of treating kids as superheroes and crushing them under the weight of expectations is common and a gross injustice to the zeners. The bottom line is: do not expect your kids to be perfect and to be good at everything, since we as adults have the same limitations.

Stop Cloning

Much like a poem loses meaning in translation, a kid loses his uniqueness in comparison. Why do we expect our kids to be clones of other kids? They are not. While appreciating another child—'Arun has got really good marks'—we often tend to add another line to it—'Why can't you score like Arun?' This second line does maximum damage. It achieves the exact opposite of what we try to achieve through the second statement. Everyone cannot earn academic honours, like everyone cannot be a sports champion; someone can sing well, others can play an instrument, still others may just be passionate about writing. Learning to appreciate their differences is the secret to discovering their uniqueness. And every child has something unique about him or her. We adults kill it by cruel comparisons.

Making It Difficult to Fail

Parents of zeners have learnt to appreciate and shower praise on their kids at the slightest of their achievements. While on the one hand this is extremely motivating, on the other, when this assumes a reason to flaunt on social media, it starts setting a trap for the child. There is no harm in sharing the achievement of your kid on social media, but then knowing how much is also important. People are obsessed with 'likes' on social media which has become a way to make oneself happy. Such branding of the child makes it difficult for him to fail in the future. The child gets trapped in this 'gift from god' image created by their parents, and hence failure becomes equivalent to shame. The child often crumbles under such pressures.

Provide, Not Pamper

Dona and Jude Pinto, parents to a ten-year-old boy and an eight-year-old girl, find this generation demanding, although they confess at the same time that besides the exposure that this generation has through media, often parents are responsible for fuelling this demanding habit. Jude recalls how influenced by a popular video channel, EvanTube, their kids went on a toy-buying spree, many of which they never played more than once or twice. Dona adds,

They are also bored very easily. As a mother to two kids, I have to plan on a daily basis new activities, new puzzles or new toys to keep them engaged. They are bored with them too soon, necessitating something new again. This can be at times exhilarating and tiring at the same time.

Learning from their experience, the message from this couple was: Provide for them, do not pamper them. We are the reason why they have not learnt to value things as much as we like them to do.

Labour of Love

Digital generation zeners have become used to getting everything at their fingertips. We as parents feel that it is important to teach them the labour of love. That is not to say that we should take their technological advantage away from them or forcibly make their lives difficult. Instead, it is to teach them the value of working hard as much as they appreciate the value of working smart.

Drone Parenting

This is an era of overzealous parenting. If millennials had helicopter parents, then zeners have drone parents. What is the difference between the two? While helicopter parents would keep hovering literally over the head of their kids and try and determine their choices, monitor them and keep a track of all their activities, drone parents have a target-driven, micro-parenting style. The parents of zeners are not able to devote as much time  to their kids; hence, they cannot be called helicopter parents, but when it comes to their career, schooling and college selection, they like target-bound drone turn out from nowhere and deliver the payload. Sumana tells how her brother who lives in the commercial capital of India—Mumbai—is already on a mission to find the best school in the city for the admission of his child while the child is still learning to walk! Parents are competitive when it comes to which school their child should study in, getting them all the facilities—better than the best. Dr Ajay Goyal, professor of organizational behaviour at a leading business school in Bengaluru, wonders why their kid's future career has become the single most obsession for most parents. This is too much of droning, so to say. Dr Ajay adds,

We do not understand that the future career of these kids may be nothing like ours. Some of the jobs that we have now may not exist in the future. As a father of a teenage boy I do not want to be obsessed with my son's future career.

I think the moment we overdo our role, it ceases to serve its true purpose. It then vitiates the whole environment, causing more harm than benefit. This obsession often leads to parents pushing their dreams and wishes on their kids. Bonshila Roy minces no words when she says,

Most parents push over their unfulfilled dreams on their kids. If a mother could not pursue a successful modelling career then she wants her daughter to pursue the same, irrespective of whether her daughter wants to do the same or not. I find this regressive and unjust and with this generation this is going to boomerang in a big way.

Nehal is from Egypt. She lives in the Kingdom of Bahrain and makes her living by working as a professor of business at a reputed university. She is a mother of three and speaks from a wealth of experience. Her eldest child is her eighteen-year-old daughter Leena, who has just finished her 12th grade and is proceeding to the USA to study digital media and photography. Her second child Omar is a fifteen-year-old boy, who has passed his 9th grade and is joining his sister in the USA to pursue further education. And her youngest child is her eight-year-old son, Murad. During the discussion with Nehal, I discovered that she had a very interesting and non-ambiguous approach towards parenting, especially when it came to career choices of her older kids. She pretty much let her kids decide their own course, guiding them wherever and whenever necessary, without dictating terms to them or imposing her own decisions on them. This has not always been easy for Nehal, since she has not felt certain about their choices and sometimes suppressed her preferences for her kids. But in no way has she stopped her kids from evolving their own thoughts and personas. Talking about her eldest daughter, she tells how a few years back Leena was completely into football and she played the game really well. She was crazy about the game and went to Spain and elsewhere to watch football matches. But then suddenly her interest shifted and despite her coaches wanting her back in the team, Leena stopped attending football practice. Leena's interest had shifted to sports media and that's what led to her deciding to study digital media and photography. Nehal recalls how, as a growing teen, Leena would show a lot of interest in her marketing subjects, often judging the advertisements and critiquing them with her mum. Nehal wants to let Leena experience what she has chosen, and she says she would be fine even if Leena decides to choose some other major as she grows up. It is important for her to let Leena find her own course and pursue her own interests. Her middle child Omar has recently won the future scientist award from his school. A popular child at his school, he has participated in various competitions including a robotics competition. Nehal says that Omar has skills to become an engineer in the future. He is good in maths and science and has the ability to pursue a career in engineering. Both she and Omar's father, who is an engineer himself, would love to see him choose engineering as a future career. However, Omar does not want to become an engineer, at least for now. He wants to study psychology in the future. I also spoke to Omar and wondered if he wanted to study psychology to know more about people and understand them. On the contrary, Omar told me that he wanted to study psychology to understand his own self. Nehal, though in her heart deeply wishes that Omar studies engineering, is not the one to force her son when it comes to making choices. When I spoke to Omar separately, he confirmed that he believed his parents would let him study psychology if he would like to do so in the future and not force him to study engineering. This is an amazingly democratic approach to parenting. What impresses me the most in this case is the fact that despite having her own set of dreams, expectations and preferences for her kids, she holds back the temptation of imposing them on her kids and lets them evolve, make their own choices, make their own mistakes, learn and find their path.

Roshini talks about how she let her daughter pursue a career of her choice, although it was unconventional.

She was very clear after her 10th grade what she wanted to do in her life. When she chose to pursue Bachelor of Arts in culinary art, I knew it was unconventional, but I let her pursue the same as I saw her conviction in making the choice.

The 3C principle

Confidence, commitment and consistency—this is the golden 3C principle I keep telling my son. I am not enamoured by the percentage of marks he gets in his exams nor will I dictate the field he chooses as his profession later on in his life. We are good if he chooses music or science, English or humanities, robotics or animation, AI or fine arts. I have told him umpteen times and keep repeating it—Whatever you do in your life, prepare only as much that makes you 'confident' in whatever you do, have enough passion so that your 'commitment' is intrinsic and remember to practise it every day; that makes you 'consistent'. I know that one day he will remember these words and embrace the '3C principle' in whatever he does in his life.

Parting Shots

By now, you as a reader must have witnessed how each chapter has been dedicated to not only understanding zeners and their life but also exploring how the different stakeholders of this generation—parents, teachers or anyone else—can connect, engage and manage them, a kind of consultative guidance, based on research and experiences. The goal is not only to create and maximize opportunities for them but more importantly to raise them as a happy and mentally healthy generation. There is no better investment than to raise them as happy functional kids who do not forget to explore, experience and experiment.

Our fireside chat is over. Arnab has finished his piano session. It is time for all three of us to hit the gym, a time that we enjoy spending together. We just lose calories; health, happiness and fun are some of the returns on investment.

Adios.

WHO IS GENERATION Z?

There is considerable confusion over the birth years and range of Generation Z. Such confusion is not new when it comes to generations, as there is no official body or governmental agency that determines generations. Generations are mostly defined by researchers and historians based on transformational changes in the environment and marked changes in attitude and behaviour of the new members of the society. Such definitions are also contextual and hence can vary slightly from one country to another, based on developmental speed, progression and advancement. All generations have faced similar conflicting definitions of their birth years. So how does one determine the most probable starting birth year of a generation? After much thought, I have concluded that there are two possible ways of doing the same: One could be to use the mathematical method of maximum frequency, that is, consider the most repeating year. In other words, the birth year that repeats maximum number of times in most of the literature is taken as the most commonly accepted. But will this create bias towards other studies? Another way could be to use the law of averages. What if we take the average of the starting year mentioned for Gen Z in various literature? This doesn't seem to be a very bad idea to me, as it does not ignore any study, in favour of the most common year.

Following are various studies and definitions of Generation Z:

S No.	Source	Year Range	Citation
1	Monster (job portal)	2000 onwards	Monster (2019)
2	Metro (UK)	2000 onwards	Lindsay (2018)
3	Pew Research Center (USA)	1997–2012	Dimock (2019)
4	Asia Business Unit of Corporate Directions, Inc.	2001–2015	Corporate Directions, Inc. (2016)
5	Philippine Retailers Association	2001 onwards	Philippine Retailers Association (2016)
6	Business Insider	1997 onwards	Premack (2018)
7	Bloomberg	2000 onwards	Mazumdar (2019)
8	Authors Meagan Johnson and Larry Johnson (*Generations, Inc.: From Boomers to Linksters—Managing the Friction between Generations at Work*)	2002 onwards	Blair (2017)
9	Author Neil Howe (*Strauss–Howe Generational Theory*)	2005–2025	Howe (2014)

We can look at these studies the way we feel it is right. If we use the maximum frequency method, then the maximum frequency of the start birth years of Generation Z is 2000. It occurs three times in the data. And even if we use the law of averages and take the average of the start birth years mentioned in these studies, then the value rounded off to nearest decimal figure is once again 2000. So no matter how we spin the above data, the year 2000 seems to be the closest correct definition as far as beginning of Generation Z is concerned. Hence, it may be safe to assume that those born in the year 2000 and after belong to Generation Z.

Akin to their birth years, they have also been called by various names—'linkster' by one author, as they are a link between the old and the new world; 'homeland generation' by another author (but it is just too American); and iGen generation by another author (Twenge, 2018). They certainly deserve a better name. Plain Generation Z is also not appealing enough. Hence, I coined a name for them that is both global and catchy at the same time. I call them 'zeners'.

Zeners, the post millennials, the preteens and teens of today make up 32 per cent of the world population (Miller & Lu, 2018), the biggest chunk of the population pie chart. They are significant today, tomorrow and thereafter. This book catches them early and decodes their attitudes, mindsets, behaviours and life realities, with an objective to become a consultative guide for anyone and everyone who manages and engages this generation. Organizations such as schools, colleges and businesses have a huge opportunity to take advantage of the demographic dividend and make a win-win proposition for everyone. Parents, teachers, counsellors, psychologists, entrepreneurs and the society in general would need this book to ensure that this generation is understood well to keep them happy and engaged, so that we all can have a better world and a better future.

References

Blair, O. (2017, 11 April). What comes after millennials? Meet the generation known as the 'linksters'. *The Independent*. Retrieved 25 July 2019, from https://www.independent.co.uk/life-style/millennials-generation-z-linksters-what-next-generation-x-baby-boomers-internet-social-media-a7677001.html

Corporate Directions, Inc. (2016, 15 March). The Thai market to watch and their players: Generation Y—the driving force of consumption

trends in Thailand. Retrieved 25 July 2019, from http://www.cdiasia
business.com/en/library/detail.html?p=299

Dimock, M. (2019, 17 January). Defining generations: Where millennials
end and Generation Z begins. Pew Research Center. Retrieved 25 July
2019,fromhttps://www.pewresearch.org/fact-tank/2019/01/17/where-
millennials-end-and-generation-z-begins/

Howe, N. (2014, 27 October). Introducing the homeland generation.
Forbes. Retrieved 25 July 2019, from https://www.forbes.com/sites/
neilhowe/2014/10/27/introducing-the-homeland-generation-part-
1-of-2/#2c01c9492bd6

Lindsay, J. (2018, 29 January). What generation am I and what do they
mean? From baby boomers to millennials. *Metro.* Retrieved 25 July
2019, from https://metro.co.uk/2018/01/29/generation-mean-baby-
boomers-millennials-7267464/

Mazumdar, R. (2019, 24 July). India running out of time to cash in on its
Gen Z boom. Bloomberg. Retrieved 25 July 2019, from https://www.
bloomberg.com/news/articles/2019-07-24/india-running-out-of-time-
to-cash-in-demographic-dividend

Miller, L. J., & Lu, W. (2018, 20 August). Gen Z is set to outnumber
millennials within a year. Bloomberg. Retrieved 25 July 2019, from
https://www.bloomberg.com/news/articles/2018-08-20/gen-z-to-
outnumber-millennials-within-a-year-demographic-trends

Monster. (2019). Watch out, millennials, Gen Z is coming to an office
near you. Retrieved 25 July 2019, from https://www.monster.com/
career-advice/article/gen-z-millennials-office-0816

Philippine Retailers Association. (2016, 21 September). Introducing the
tech-savvy Generation Z. Retrieved 24 July 2019, from http://www.
philretailers.com/introducing-the-tech-savvy-generation-z/

Premack, R. (2018, 12 July). Millennials love their brands, Gen Zs are terrified
of college debt, and 6 other ways Gen Zs and millennials are totally
different. Business Insider. Retrieved 24 July 2019, from https://www.
businessinsider.com/gen-zs-habits-different-from-millennials-2018-6

Twenge, J. M. (2018). *iGen: Why today's super-connected kids are growing
up less rebellious, more tolerant, less happy—and completely unprepared
for adulthood—and what that means for rest of us.* New York, NY:
Atria Books.

ABOUT THE AUTHOR

Debashish Sengupta, a dual PhD, completed his PhD in management from Central University of Nicaragua (UCN) and Azteca University, Mexico. He holds certificates in 'Social Psychology' and 'Leadership Development' from Wesleyan University, USA, and Japan Management Association, respectively. He is an award-winning author. His book *The Life of Y: Engaging Millennials as Employees and Consumers* (SAGE Publications) recently won the first prize at the DMA-NTPC Management Book Awards—a national-level award in India. The book has not only become a bestseller, but it has also been featured in the library collections by Stanford University. Dr Sengupta is also the co-author of the Crossword Bestseller and KPMG-cited book *Employee Engagement*. He has authored five other acclaimed books. His research papers have been published in leading international journals. His papers have featured in leading international journals including *TQR (The Qualitative Report)*; *International Journal of Learning Management Systems*; *PM World Journal*; *Journal of Project, Program & Portfolio Management*; and *Journal of Business and Retail Management Research* to name a few. Besides this, he has written for numerous business media publications and has over 100 publications to his credit. Recently, he was featured globally as the 'author of the week' by *PM World Journal*, USA, to honour his research contributions. He occasionally writes for reputed business media publications. He has received several research awards in his career spanning over two decades, including best paper awards and young researcher award.

Dr Sengupta is the Asia Editor of a London-based leading global business magazine *The Future of Earth: Environment, Economy and Society*. He is a much-sought-after speaker, trainer and business consultant to various Indian and multinational companies. His strategic and practical insights guide leaders of large and small organizations worldwide, through his teaching, writing and direct consultation to major corporations and governments.

Dr Sengupta presently teaches human resource and strategy at the Royal University for Women Bahrain. He has teaching experience spanning nearly two decades and has taught students from India, the USA, Europe and Far East.

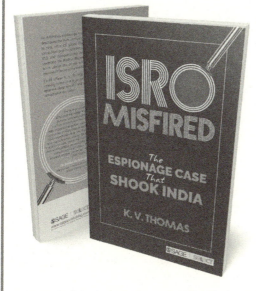

Made in the USA
Monee, IL
02 April 2022